CHILDREN AS READERS

A study

John Spink

CHILDREN AS READERS

A study

John Spink

CLIVE BINGLEY  LONDON

Published by
Library Association Publishing Limited
7 Ridgmount Street
London WC1E 7AE

First published 1989

British Library Cataloguing in Publication Data

Spink, John
  Children as readers: a study.
  1. Children. Reading skills. Development
  I. Title
  428.4'3

  ISBN 0-85157-440-8

•

Typeset in 10/12pt Times by Library Association Publishing Ltd.
Printed and made in Great Britain by Redwood Burn Ltd,
Trowbridge, Wilts.

Dedicated to the memory of

JOHN PARIS

who knew what he was doing

Contents

Introduction

The purpose of this book is not only to fill a gap in the literature but also to provide a text that is both academically sound and readable. Its aim is to bring together a number of topics that have been discussed in the areas of literary theory, of child psychology, and of children's literature. It is not intended as a substitute for the reading of, say, Nicholas Tucker's *The child and the book* (1981) or Margaret Meek's *Learning to read* (1982), but rather as a guide towards such readings. The references and further reading given at the ends of chapters are there to be used. The ideas discussed here are intended to be tested against your own experiences as librarian, teacher, or parent of real children.

It is easy to become so fascinated by theories (especially theories that tidy up the messiness and uncertainties of life as experienced) that we suspend that protective scepticism that gives us a sense of reality. The danger sign of this departure from reality, and often from common sense, is the use of the concept of 'the child'. 'The child' is an abstraction, a generalization, and often an idealization. 'The child' of textbooks and romantic literature usually performs better, more reasonably, and more agreeably than the children we know. If the children we know are 'our own' (users of our services, or our school-class, or—worse—our offspring) accounts of 'the child' can be very disheartening. This being so, I will try to avoid 'the child'—this wonderful standard product—and instead talk about children. Children come in a variety of shapes, sizes, and colours and are consistently inconsistent, predictably unpredictable. They are the subject of this book.

This book is also about reading. As you will discover (if you progress to chapter 1), I will not only be concerned with the reading of books and other printed materials but also with the reading of sounds and images. I might thus have chosen to call this book *Children as readers of texts, listeners to sounds, and viewers of pictures*. I rejected this title since it seemed to lack a certain succinctness, but the broad approach it indicates has been retained.

Most books concerned with reading have one or two chapters on reading difficulties, dyslexia, reluctant readers, and so on. There is a vast literature concerned exclusively with these matters (perhaps there are more books about digestive disorders than there are about the appreciation of eating and drinking). This is rather depressing. It was Margaret M. Clark in her study, *Young fluent readers* (1976), who redressed the balance as far as reading studies are concerned. She reminded us that the behaviour of competent readers is as interesting and illuminating as that of poor and unwilling readers. In the present book I am mainly concerned with the competent reader although, as a former member of that group, I will also show concern for children with reading problems.

There is one other element of my approach I hope will remain with the reader. This is the realization that 'reading' is just one of many activities among children—just one of many ways of obtaining information, understanding, and enjoyment. It seems wrong, therefore, to treat it in isolation or to suggest that it is separate from (some would argue *superior to*) other activities. The child who is at this moment sitting reading a book will soon be watching television, playing hockey or soccer, arguing and fighting, or watching and listening to parents, peers, and even teachers. All that is learnt in this variety of interactions affects how we grow. It is a life-long process and much of it is deeply enjoyable.

As I have already indicated, I hope that this book will prove to be useful to a readership wider than members of the library profession. Librarians in schools and public libraries are fully aware of the importance of reading. Those serving young people in public libraries have agreed (Heeks and Turner, 1981) that their basic objectives are

1 to promote an awareness of the pleasures afforded by books and related materials;
2 to assist language development;
3 to promote the acceptance of books and related materials as fundamental means of meeting information needs; and
4 to extend and deepen cultural awareness.

However, these objectives are shared by most people who are concerned with the growth and development of young people—teachers, parents, and so on. For these reasons most of the chapters of this book should have a wide interest.

Chapters 1 and 2 establish what we mean when we speak of 'reading' and of 'development'. Chapter 3 attempts to show how reading can affect various kinds of physical and mental development. Reading depends upon the ability to obtain meaning from print and from pictures, and so Chapter 4 is concerned with how we learn to read print, and Chapter 5 with how we read pictorial material. Chapter 6 concentrates on reading materials and discusses the qualities of 'good books'.

Chapters 7 and 8 (though mainly concerned with the work of the professional librarian) should contain something of interest to those who work with young people and who organize services and activities for and with them. The final chapter, Chapter 9, returns to general issues that concern us all.

Who was John Paris, to whom this book is dedicated? He was a schoolmaster in a Merseyside school who, faced with a collection of unlovely and unpromising-looking boys—great louts who had outgrown their desks as their voices had broken—somehow retained his faith in the power of literature. He successfully guided us (the all-revealing 'us'!) through the 'set books' and then did something far more intimate and rather courageous, considering its potential for disaster: he read to us 'for pleasure'. He read the books *he* enjoyed. On Friday afternoons he defied the dictatorial syllabus and read *Kidnapped*, *Tom Sawyer*, *Huckleberry Finn*, and, rather incongruously, the Wee Macgreegor stories of J. T. Bell. In the process he showed us the deep and personal pleasure that comes with the bringing together of the right book and the right reader. So that was what it was all about, all this rather unrevealing talk about 'the greatness of literature'! John Paris's version of 'Beauty and the beasts', his act of cultural defiance, has kept me 'powered' for half a century.

Many of us have been greatly advantaged by meeting a John Paris, a patient and understanding schoolteacher or librarian, by having well-read parents and friends who have pushed the right book our way. Some of us have had the educational advantage of working with bright pupils and students keen to share the pleasure of novels and poems (and TV programmes and cinema and theatre) with us.

I suggest that we are concerned with supporting the already-competent and adventurous reader, but particularly with the disadvantaged: those who have not been fired with delight, who have not learned to enjoy, who have never been guided towards *their* book, or encouraged to listen to a particular piece of music, or introduced to a particular TV programme. It is one of the roles of the teacher, the librarian, and the parent to act as a John Paris to those who 'never had a chance'.

A note on one of the words I often use. When I use the word 'parent' I will be indicating anyone assuming a parental role—from a temporary baby-sitter to long-term foster-parents, from 'natural' parents to teachers and librarians working with children.

Finally, the most pleasant part of an introduction for the author: the acknowledgements. This book has been an opportunity to repay a little of my debt to the library profession, particularly to individuals to whom I owe gratitude for help and friendship willingly given, and tasks willingly shared. I need to stress, however, that any faults and failings in the text are 'all my own work'; many of the successful elements are the result of help and advice from others.

I should specifically like to acknowledge the help of a number of individuals, particularly my colleagues, Dr Kevin McGarry, Ray Lonsdale, and Malcolm Tunley, whose friendship and professional support are constantly appreciated. Kate Snowdon, of Hertfordshire County Library, read all the chapters as they were written. She sustained me with her enthusiasm and the quality (and spirit) of her comments. Thanks, too, to Judith Bater of Bristol Polytechnic, who kept me 'in touch' on a number of points. Barbara Jones and her colleagues in Knowsley Public Library Service cast an experienced eye over Chapter 7. My wife, Siân, read the final draft and made useful comments and encouraging noises at the right moment. I am also grateful to June Jones, who helped with the proofs. I owe a particular debt to one group of people, my former students at the College of Librarianship, Wales. Finally, I wish to thank Megan, Dafydd, and Huw for their loving interest and help. I particularly appreciate the use of Megan's 'library'.

A former student of mine, a refreshingly direct and perceptive young woman, once came to consult me about a course I was offering. She asked a range of exploratory questions before she came round to the crucial one. 'Was the subject', she asked, 'waffley?' This book considers a number of subjects that give rise to much flannel, fudge, and wild speculation. I hope that it doesn't prove to be too 'waffley'.

References and further reading
1 Clark, Margaret M. (1976) *Young fluent readers: what can they teach us?*, London, Heinemann Educational Books.
2 Heeks, Peggy, and Turner, Paul (eds.) (1981) *Public library aims and objectives: policy statements prepared by members of the Public Libraries Research Group*, London, Public Libraries Research Group.
3 Meek, Margaret (1982) *Learning to read*, London, The Bodley Head.
4 Tucker, Nicholas (1981) *The child and the book: a psychological and literary exploration*, Cambridge University Press.

1

What is reading?

Definitions

What is reading?—a simple question to which one would expect a simple answer. In the event one finds a range of immediate answers, each one of which is too simple to reveal or even adequate to explain what soon emerges as a complex process: 'Reading is a creation of the sound form of the word on the basis of its graphic reproduction' (the Russian educationist, El'konin, 1973, p.552); 'Reading is a complex process by which a reader reconstructs, to some degree, a message encoded by a writer in graphic language' (Goodman and Niles, 1970, p.5); 'Reading involves nothing more than the correlation of a sound image with its corresponding visual image' (Bloomfield, quoted in Harris and Hodges, 1981, p.264).

The limitation of these simple answers is that they suggest that the reader has a relatively, if not completely, passive role. The writer 'encodes' a message, employing graphic signs, and the reader unravels, or rather 'decodes' that message. A competent reader regains the total message of a competent writer.

This model might be seen to suffice as a description of the new reader's performance: 'Here is the boy. Here is the girl. Here is the dog. Here is ... ' with terrible predictability, 'the ball.' But as we shall see, even this is to be questioned.

What the model does is to suggest at least two things that need to be examined critically. The first, as already noted, is the idea of the neutrality of the reader. The other is the writer's expectation of, and perhaps preference for, the reader's neutrality.

As we know by experience, readers are not neutral or passive. They worry what they are reading like terriers. The human mind is usually so active that it sets off a number of 'what if?' speculations and 'is that really so?' evaluations under the stimulation of the text. It is the kind of rapid, critical examination to which we expose another person when we encounter them for the first time. We employ a whole set of ideas, values, and other associations—the rewards of our life experience—to the task.

1

If the foregoing suggests the activity of experienced adult readers, let us look at that most basic, apparently neutral, and certainly most mundane, of sentences: 'The cat sat on the mat'. Here it is possible for the jaded adult reader to treat the sentence passively, particularly as he or she can deal in generalizations ('cat', 'mat'). It is at least possible that many young children would view 'the cat' as a quite specific cat—the family cat, Simon's cat, Grandma's cat. Thus 'the cat' becomes an elderly, spiteful, ginger cat, or whatever.

Even for the reader who can generalize, it is difficult to be objective about something like a cat. It is difficult to avoid bringing one's own associations to such an idea. Some people associate cats with warmth, friendliness, softness, comfort, the domestic scene, and the home. Others associate cats with the sinister, the slinky, the secretive, the sly—'Aaughh!' as Charlie Brown would say.

Note, also, the cultural factor operating here. This view of cats is shared by people who have, and who can perhaps afford to have, the idea of 'animals as pets'. In some societies it might be possible, indeed usual, to be neutral about cats. In a similar way, 'mat' might be a neutral word for you—unless, perhaps, you are a member of the Islamic faith when it may be associated with your religious observances, or (at a lower level) you may have just lost a great deal of money in an investment in floor coverings! In this kind of discussion it is necessary to distinguish between cultural, shared associations, and associations specific to the individual person.

It is clear that reading is a dynamic activity in which the reader is actively involved—that it has much to do with the reader's thought processes. Wolfgang Iser (1974, p.288) has provided us with a picture of the competent reader's behaviour, for—as he says—when we read 'we look forward, we look back, we decide, we change our decisions, we form expectations, we are shocked by their nonfulfilment, we question, we muse, we accept, we reject'.

This competent reader does not have to be an adult: much of this activity takes place when adult and child, or child and child, or child and teddy bear explore a picture book. What is Rosie doing? What is the fox trying to do? Will the fox eat Rosie? What if the fox hadn't stepped on the rake? What did Rosie have for her dinner? The speculation extends from the obvious (the 'whodunit?') to the more searching (the 'why did he-or-she dunit?').

Recent definitions and descriptions of the reading process have acknowledged and helped to explain its complexity: 'Reading is a way of arriving at ideas by looking at print. It is an activity concerned with *meaning*' (Kennedy, 1984, p.146); 'Reading is not just a matter of transfer

2

of information from the print to the reader's mind, there is also an active contribution from the reader's store of knowledge. We bring our own experience to bear on what is being read by filling gaps, by interpretation, and by extrapolating from what is given in the text' (Crowder, 1982, p.137).

Thus reading is seen as something like 'thinking under the stimulus of print', with the reader—rather than the text—being at the core of the process:

> Reading involves the recognition of printed or written symbols which serve as stimuli for recall of meanings built up through past experience, and the construction of new meanings through manipulation of concepts already possessed by the reader. The resulting meanings are organized into thought processes according to the purposes adopted by the reader. Such an organization leads to new behaviour which takes its place, either in personal or in social development.
>
> (Tinker and McCullough, quoted in Downing, 1972, pp.30−1)

No one has stressed the role of the reader, the centrality of the reader, more than Frank Smith (1985, p.49), who says that 'Readers must bring meaning *to* print rather than expect to receive meaning *from* it'. What does all of this mean for the teacher or librarian promoting reading and the use of books and similar materials? It means that we are not only working to enable children to have access to information, knowledge, and literature (with or without a capital letter) but that we are also helping them to develop critical and independent thinking. We are helping the individual, whether adult or young person, to gain meaning from the vast display of information, opinion, and activity that constitutes our daily lives. The alternative to 'gaining meaning' is to be overwhelmed, to lose individuality, and to lose control.

A model of the reading process

From the above discussion it is apparent that the usual model of the communication process is inadequate to describe the complexity of the reading process. A typical model, considered by some to be applicable in any communication situation, would take the following form:

Transmitter	⟶	Message	⟶	Receiver
Perceives				Receives
Encodes				Decodes
Transmits				Responds

3

Thus the person, the sender, perceives the need to send a message, encodes it into the appropriate form—a written poem, a telephone message, a face-to-face verbal message—and transmits it. The transmission may be simple, the shout 'You are standing on my foot!' or a phone conversation, or it may be complicated, as in the example of this book, involving a variety of people who are employed in the publishing, printing, and bookselling businesses. The person who receives the message as a phone call, a letter, a printed book, or a shout, receives the message perfectly or imperfectly, decodes it, and reacts in some way. It is the complexity of the decoding and responding that seems to be under-represented in this model, as can be seen in the communication model if the following is substituted:

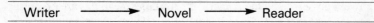

In the early 1960s a distinguished American educationist, William S. Gray, offered another kind of model of the reading process. This has much to commend it, since it recognizes both the complexity of the reading process and the varieties of reader behaviours.

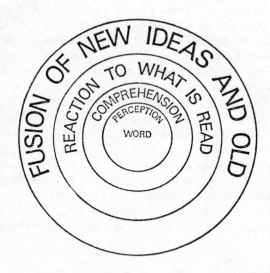

Fig. 1.1   Gray's model of the major components of reading (Clymer, 1972, p.61)

At the centre of the process is the act of perception, perception of the words. If we are concerned with readers who have sensory deprivation, or if we are confronted with unfamiliar alphabets—in the writer's case examples of these would be Arabic or Japanese—there may be much preparation before the process can continue. It may mean learning an unfamiliar alphabet or a whole language. It may involve the use of mechanical aids, such as eye-glasses, or the conversion of one medium into another, for example, the production of 'talking books'.

Comprehension level is attained when the reader not only decodes the words but also understands what the words are saying. At the early stages of learning to read, some children have to struggle so hard to convert symbols into sounds that they do not gain meaning: 'Teh—Heh—Th—Eh—Theh—THE—Cee—Keh—Ah—Teh—CAT—The cat', and so forth. Modern methods of teaching reading avoid this stage, as is shown in Chapter 4.

Under certain circumstances, reading goes little beyond this level of comprehension. The reading undertaken while under stress—while waiting for the dentist, for example, or while sitting in a plane during turbulence, or when fatigued at the end of the day—is usually of this order. The alert and attentive reader, however, usually brings critical attention to what is being read and reacts in some way. One set of reactions is concerned with our acceptance or rejection of the book, regardless of the author's hopes and intentions. What we are reading may invite reaction: Shirley Hughes expects us to react to Dave's loss of Dogger and to be concerned about the problem of Alfie when he is locked inside the house.* Many books invite us to explore a subject (insects, knights in armour, acid rain) or to engage in some activity like playing hockey or using a computer.

Much that we read does not seem to affect us very much—if at all. Some of the things we read cause us to gain knowledge and understanding, to question and to reconsider already-held 'knowledge' and opinions. Occasionally we read material that causes us to change our view of the world fundamentally, our way of life. This level of activity is labelled by Gray (1960, p.10) as a 'fusion of new ideas and old'. He would have been the first person to agree that this is an inadequate label for a process in which some sets of ideas are restructured and some are rejected. At one level this is what happens when we refine our perception of concepts such as 'insects' (from which everything small that creeps or crawls to

---

*Further details about the children's books to which passing reference is made in the text are to be found in the brief reading list at the end of the book.

the more precise 'creatures with six legs and bodies consisting of three elements: body, thorax, and head') or 'the Victorian age', or 'freedom'. At another level this also happens when we commit ourselves to a particular religion or ideology.

It is perhaps once again necessary to remind ourselves that we are not merely concerned with the behaviour of adults. These processes are taking place in the minds of young readers while they are widening their world of ideas, knowledge, and understanding, of faith and belief. They are taking place when the youngest reader sits with a picture-book or, better, shares a picture-book.

Factors affecting reader reception

Reading is not as simple as it seems, and the reader is not as passive a receiver as we once thought. Gray (Clymer, 1972, p.61) has shown that the competent reader has the ability 'to read the lines, to read between the lines, and to read beyond the lines'. That is, the reader reads what is stated, and reads what is implied. The reader also extends the author's ideas, using his or her own knowledge, experience, and so on.

Although a group of children or adults may read the same text, it is likely that each person will gain a different 'reading' and will respond to the shared text in different ways. What kinds of factors bring about this individuality of response?

Degree of reading competence

The individual's ability to 'process' print includes basic reading skills and the more specialized skills required by a particular kind of text. The development of reading competence is a life-long process for the competent 'general' reader, who may still have to learn how to read, for example, a scientific, theological, or legal text. Children may find it easy to read a straightforward narrative text but may, for example, have difficulty with broken unity, with a mixture of everyday reality and magic, or with a text requiring some understanding of historical chronology. A given text may demand a kind of reading for which we are not yet prepared. Hence comes the importance of teaching reading throughout a child's school career and beyond.

The 'reading circumstances'

This means the time and situation in which reading takes place. Under some circumstances reading becomes a superficial activity: reading when we are tired or unwell. On other occasions we become efficient readers, as when we are approaching an examination or want to learn to do something quickly. Some reading requires quiet and calm; some reading cries out to be shared, perhaps to be read aloud.

Under this heading we might also include the reader's stage of development in terms of experience and education. Some books are encountered before we are ready for them, for example, before we can engage with the characters. Some books are encountered too late, after the period when they would have had maximum impact. The writer discovered or was introduced to *Robinson Crusoe* too early, so that it appeared to be a tedious book; Mervyn Peake's Gormenghast trilogy appeared a little too late, so that he accepted it with a little less excitement than it deserved; and Proust's *Remembrance of things past* came at the right moment when he had the tenacity for the task. One of the arts of the parent, the teacher, and the librarian is to ensure that the right book is in the right hands at the right moment. This is a fine art and the rewards are considerable.

The reader's relationship with the author

Much of the success or failure of our engagement with a book depends upon our response to the persona of the author, that is, the character the author assumes in the book. It may not, of course, be the full, real character of the author him- or herself.

As with people we meet during the day, some authors are accepted as close friends while others alienate or repel us. It is very much a matter of personal reaction and of personal taste. The factors involved are subtle ones of tone of voice, attitudes to characters, and touches that suggest friendliness or superiority. A young reader would perhaps define an attractive author as one with whom he or she would like to spend a day. Consider the personae of Arthur Ransome, E. Nesbit, and Enid Blyton, and in this same light the writers of information books.

The competent and experienced reader can overcome an initial resistance to an author with irritating mannerisms; the young reader probably needs to feel sympathy or empathy in order to engage with an author.

The reader's expectation

Expectations are built up by past experience of an author's books, by a title, by the book's dust-jacket, and by its illustrations. Less obvious factors, such as type size and page layout, will affect the young reader who may dismiss a book as 'a baby's book' or as 'a hard book' on the impression given by such elements.

Expectation is sometimes frustrated, as when an author tries something new or when a liberally-illustrated book turns out to be unexciting. Some authors, of course, frustrate expectation in exciting ways. What will Roald Dahl, Raymond Briggs, or the Ahlbergs do next? Not what we expect. Indeed, the unexpected becomes our expectation in these cases.

The reader's background knowledge

Every author makes certain assumptions about his or her reader and expects a degree of knowledge, understanding, and experience. An author may expect his or her reader to have at least a general idea of when the Vikings lived, or what it feels like to be bullied, or to be able to cope with simple scientific concepts, or to know the general geography of the USA. In specific areas such as space exploration, computer science, and popular music, an author can expect many young readers to have a considerable (not to say a remarkable) amount of existing knowledge. It would be a foolhardy author who assumed that Young Reader automatically meant Uninformed Reader.

The reader's own experience and associations

These are the elements that will enable the reader to engage with a book in a personal way and develop the text from individual experience and understanding. Clearly, if a reader has had the experience of a holiday in France, or a visit to a factory, or of owning a pet, or of experiencing the death of a loved person or animal, this direct experience will be brought to a story or information book dealing with the same matters.

It should be possible to relate the reader's personality traits to the kind of response the reader will make to a particular story or information book. There is a danger of over-simplification here, especially if one forgets that such traits as introvert/extrovert and optimist/pessimist are, at best, rough indications—they are continua, not two set points. It is perhaps possible to say that a particular child tends towards introversion and, further, that he or she is therefore more likely to engage with characters such as Tom in Philippa Pearce's *Tom's midnight garden*, Max in Pauline Clarke's *The twelve and the genii*, or Tolly in Lucy Boston's Green Knowe stories, than a more extrovert reader. It is also possible to argue that less sensitive and reflective young readers might prefer Astrid Lindgren's Pippi Longstocking stories, or relate to Erica in Jan Mark's *Handles* rather than to the solitary Toms, Maxes, and Tollies.

Merely to embark on such an approach reveals how inadequate and simplistic it is. Human beings are more complex than this exercise will allow. A young person has changing moods and changing needs—not merely at different stages of development but at different times of the day. So-called 'introverted' children have their 'extrovert' moments and even very active children must have quiet, reflective periods.

The final point to be made is that the whole reading experience takes place within a particular cultural setting, and this will affect reception. For example, it is sometimes difficult, when sitting in a British home or school, to appreciate fully the attitudes and motivation of characters, the humour, or even the value system in a Russian folk-tale or a story of modern life in Tokyo. There may, of course, be a domestic culture that is distinct from the school or street culture. Children who have, for example, a Jewish, Hindu, Welsh, or Irish home in an English town or city often have the advantage of sharing two or more cultures that can enrich each other and that can help to spread understanding in the community.

The reader and the text

From the above it is evident that the quality of a reading experience does not relate entirely to the quality of the reading material, but that it partly relates to those things the reader *brings to the text*. Indeed, many authors expect and require the reader to bring something to the text. The usual example given is that of Laurence Sterne who, in his extravaganza, *Tristram Shandy*, first published in 1760−7, stated that

> As no one, who knows what he is about in good company, would venture to talk all;—so no author, who understands the just boundaries of decorum and good breeding, would presume to think all: The truest respect which you can pay to the reader's understanding, is to halve this matter amicably, and leave him something to imagine, in his turn, as well as yourself. For my own part, I am eternally paying him compliments of this kind, and do all that lies in my power to keep his imagination as busy as my own.   (Sterne, 1760−7, p.127)

Later writers have voiced the same view. Henry James, for example, has said that with a good story 'the reader does quite half the labour' (quoted in Booth, 1987, pp.49−50) and around this idea has developed the theory of 'tell-tale gaps'. (For a clear explanation of tell-tale gaps, see Chambers, 1977.) The author, consciously or unconsciously, leaves elements for the reader to provide. It is for this reason that we sometimes 'know' details about a character that the author, we are surprised to find, has not given us. This sometimes emerges when we find a book illustration, or a film or television interpretation, unconvincing. It does not match up to the image the writer and the reader have created together. Young readers are at least as good as older readers at this process of 'realization'—and are usually more ready to challenge interpretations by illustrators, actors, or story-tellers as 'wrong'.

The above argument does not, of course, invalidate the evaluation of materials for use by children. It does, however, encourage caution—and humility. The potential for a reader's motivation, involvement, and reward can be seen in books like Raymond Briggs' *The snowman* (with its many

9

tell-tale gaps since it has no text) and Susan Cooper's *The dark is rising* novels. Prediction has been shown to be difficult, if not dangerous, when one thinks of all those worthy, well-written, sincerely felt, and critically-supported books that remain unread (see Manning, 1969; Avery, 1972), and those obvious, apparently superficial and mundane pot-boilers that gain young readers' affections.

Reading and the unconscious
It may be considered that the theories so far discussed have failed to recognize the intensity and the intimacy felt when the right young reader and the right book come together. The right book becomes something passionately possessed ('mine!'), something that cannot be read too often, the text being treated with an almost academic concern for accuracy. Even the attentive parent may wonder why P. D. Eastman's *Are you my mother?* or the current number of *The Dandy* has such a hold over their child. It is clear that the stories are meeting some real, deep, need but one rarely has clues as to what that need may be or as to what is happening in the reader.

Past studies of reading concentrated on *the text* and paid little attention to the reader who was engaged with it. William S. Gray's model (1972), while stressing the reader rather than the text, did not really begin to provide insights beyond the intellectual activity of the reader. It was left to the psychoanalytical approach to explore the emotional element in reading.

Norman Holland's theory of reading (1975) takes as its starting point *the text*, but the text as perceived by the individual reader. In his carefully worked-through interpretation of the reader's behaviour, he identifies two sets of activity. In the first, largely-conscious activity, the reader engages intellectually with various themes in the text to find a central meaning. In the second (more profound and unconscious), the reader engages with certain associations that appear to be personal to the reader and that come together as one, central fantasy. He goes on to argue that these fantasies are not as personal, not as individual as at first appears, since they are such fundamental, childhood fantasies as castration fears, oedipal fears, and so on.

Holland thus leads us to a dynamic and important role of reading: 'The psychoanalytic theory of literature holds that the writer expresses and disguises childhood fantasies. The reader unconsciously elaborates the fantasy content of the literary work with his own versions of these fantasies .... And it is the management of these fantasies, both his own and the work's, that permits their partial gratification and gives literary pleasure' (1975, p.52).

Holland is not specifically concerned with children's reading, although the basis of his work is childhood experience. Margaret and Michael Rustin are among others who have applied psychoanalytic approaches to children's fiction. In their *Narratives of love and loss* (1987, pp.1–2) they have set out 'to understand and ... explain the astonishing emotional depth and moving power of works which might at first sight appear deceptively simple to adult readers, written as they are to be read by children'.

Although one may feel an initial resistance to the bases of psychoanalysis, it clearly provides a unique means of examining the emotional impact of children's books. It receives further consideration in the next chapter.

Extending the idea of 'reading' beyond print

This book is mainly concerned with obtaining meaning from the printed and pictorial material in books, but it would be a mistake to disregard the other common media of indirect experience. Young people's needs for information, understanding, and entertainment are not only met by books but also by television programmes, by cinema films, and by recorded sound. If we are concerned with obtaining meaning from symbols and images, it follows that we should be concerned with this wide range of media.

Indeed, there is a whole range of 'reading' that is more basic than that already considered and that is crucially important in human lives. This is the reading of the status, attitudes, and moods of our fellow beings and of their activities. 'I read you' we say and we 'read' (or attempt to read) such things as football and hockey games. Unfortunately, in a book of this size it is not possible to deal with all aspects of obtaining meaning from symbols and images. The way we read people—using body language, and so on—deserves a book to itself.

Another important field that will not receive the attention it deserves in this book is the whole area of music. We have a limited understanding of the way people listen to and enjoy various kinds of music, and how we 'read' it with the ears. Sometimes dismissed as a fringe activity ('an educational frill'), listening to music is clearly as important to as many children as it is to many adults. Far from being a luxury or a peripheral activity, music often meets basic needs: 'There exist a good many people for whom music is so important that it is difficult for them to conceive of life without it. Indeed, some would say, without much exaggeration, that, were they to be deprived of music, life would lose its meaning' (Storr, 1970, p.363).

In the light of this, and with an awareness of the youngest children's enjoyment of sounds and rhythms and the early emergence of musical talent, it is regrettable that music receives little attention here. It deserves full and separate treatment, but the reader will no doubt keep it in mind as a major aspect of children's emotional lives.

References and further reading

Avery, Gillian (1972), 'In and out of fashion', *The Times literary supplement*, 28 April, no.3661, pp.473–4.

Booth, Wayne C. (1987) *The rhetoric of fiction*, Harmondsworth: Penguin, 2nd edn.

Chambers, Aidan (1977) 'The reader in the book . . . ', *Signal*, no.23, pp.76–8.

Clymer, Theodore (1972) 'What is "reading"?: some current concepts', in Amelia Melnik and John Merritt (eds.) for the Open University's Reading Development course, *Reading: today and tomorrow*, London: University of London Press/Open University, © 1972 The Open University Press. (For a clear account of Gray's theories and the development of his model, see Gray below.

Crowder, Robert G. (1982) *The psychology of reading: an introduction*, Oxford University Press.

Downing, John (1972) 'The meaning of "reading"', *Reading*, Vol. 6, no. 3, pp.30–1.

El'konin, D. B. (1973) 'USSR', in John Downing (ed.) *Comparative reading: cross-national studies of behavior and processes in reading and writing*, New York: Macmillan, pp.551–79.

Goodman, Kenneth S., and Niles, Olive S. (1970) *Reading: process and program*, Champaign, Ill.: Commission on the English Curriculum/National Council of Teachers of English.

Gray, William S. (1960) 'The major aspects of reading', in Helen M. Robinson (ed.) *Sequential development of reading abilities*, report of 1960 conference on reading, University of Chicago, University of Chicago Press, Supplementary Educational Monograph, no.90.

Harris, Theodore L., and Hodges, Richard E. (eds.) *A dictionary of reading and related terms*, Newark, Del.: International Reading Association.

Holland, Norman N. (1975) *The dynamics of literary response*, New York: W. W. Norton Library.

Iser, Wolfgang (1974) *The implied reader: patterns of communication in prose fiction from Bunyan to Beckett*, Baltimore: Johns Hopkins University Press.

Kennedy, Alan (1984) *The psychology of reading*, London: Methuen.

Manning, Rosemary (1969) 'Whatever happened to Onion John?', *The Times literary supplement*, 4 Dec., no.3536, pp.1383–4.

Rustin, Margaret, and Rustin, Michael (1987) *Narratives of love and loss: studies in modern children's fiction*, London: Verso.

Smith, Frank (1985) *Reading*, Cambridge University Press, 2nd edn.

Sterne, Laurence (1760–7 (1986)) *The life and opinions of Tristram Shandy, Gentleman*, Harmondsworth: Penguin.

Storr, Anthony (1970) 'The meaning of music', *The Times literary supplement*, 20 Nov., no.3586.

2

Theories of development

Direct and indirect experience

Jean Jacques Rousseau published his theory of education, *Émile*, in 1762 and—although Voltaire (Morrish, p.85) dismissed it as a 'hodge podge of silly wet nurse in four parts'—it is still read and still has influence today. Among other things, Rousseau (*ibid*.) stresses the importance of direct experience in the education of children: 'Children soon forget what they say or what is said to them, but not what they have done nor what has been done to them'; 'Give your scholar no verbal lessons; he should be taught by experience only' (*ibid*. p.56); 'I do not like verbal explanations. Young people pay little heed to them, nor do they remember them. Things! Things! .... We lay too much stress upon words; we teachers babble, and our scholars follow our example' (*ibid*. p.143).

In the light of this distrust in the effectiveness of verbal instruction, what was Rousseau's opinion of reading? It was a predictably low one: 'Reading is the curse of childhood' (*ibid*. p.80); 'The child who reads ceases to think, he only reads' (*ibid*. p.131); 'I hate books: they only teach us to talk about things we know nothing about' (*ibid*. p.147).

One sees the need to be reminded of the richness of direct experience, especially today when so much is learnt and experienced indirectly from print, printouts, and television. Rousseau's case, however, is overstated. He overlooks the role of reading when direct experience is not possible and when it is not desirable. For example, it is difficult to have direct experience of the past, or of present-day life in far-off parts of the world. Artefacts help to bring vividness to understanding but they need considerable explanation to make them really meaningful. This is particularly so for those children—and for those adults, including the present writer—who have an imperfect grasp of chronology. Examples of the finest artwork of a particular moment in time or place can give a false impression since they exclude reference to those living on a different level of existence. They give some impression of the life and environment of the wealthy and influential but cause one to forget, or overlook, the lives of the majority of people living at a lower level of survival—a majority that probably includes the makers of the art object. The particular richness of the *Mary Rose* findings was not in the rare 'art' objects so much as in the wealth of objects used in everyday Tudor life. Stress on rural artefacts, particularly those produced for tourists, can leave children with the impression that there are no modern industries, no modern transport, and no cities in Africa, India, and so on.

Similarly, although it may be felt necessary for children to have some understanding of violence (trench warfare; personal violence; the physical, visual, and verbal violence of city life), one would wish children to be spared the direct experience of it. Many, of course, are not, and that would seem to increase the need for the advantaged children to be given some understanding of the harsh world in which many other children have to live. Physical and mental ill-health, social disadvantage, and racial disadvantage are other areas that might be cited as examples.

There is also the element of preparing for some of life's experiences: for the first visit to the dentist or to hospital; for coping with separation from parents or with death. There are less traumatic events in life that can be quite as overwhelming or perplexing without some form of preparation—a visit to an airport or a dairy farm; first experiments with make-up and fashion; and first dates and discos. No books or videos are likely to be totally adequate to prepare one, for example, for the first day at 'big' school, but they may provide some insights and 'structures' so that the experience is not overwhelming.

Rousseau misses the point that direct experience is often inadequate *as* direct experience: an actual motor-car engine, even one that can be taken apart, does not really explain how internal combustion powers a car. Seeing the Houses of Parliament, or even a debate in the Chamber, does not explain how we are governed. Indirect experience, through diagrams, film sequences, and similar means, helps to explain and to structure what we experience directly. A room full of animals is bewildering until we are introduced to the idea of sets (categories of living creatures). A symphony is a mass of pleasant, or unpleasant, sounds until someone explains its structure. A keen apiarist, standing among the hives, will soon have to produce a piece of paper and a pencil if he or she is going to explain bee behaviour to a group of children.

Rousseau (1762, p.147) did approve of one book: 'This is the first book Émile will read; for a long time it will form his whole library and it will always retain an honoured place. It will be the text to which all talks about natural science are but the commentary'. Bearing in mind Rousseau's educational approach, and the date of *Émile*, perhaps you can guess the name of this book.*

Here again Rousseau fails to make the point that books can provide what is (because of the writer's art and craft) virtually a direct experience. His favoured writer had the skills to transport the reader so that he or she felt, smelt, and heard whatever he intended. Other writers have created fantasy worlds—Lilliput, Wonderland, Oz, Middle Earth, Gormenghast, Animal Farm—that are so vivid that, for a time, they exist. Any reader of any age can instance passages in books that were so convincing, so moving, that they were almost direct experiences.

Acknowledging, then, the value of direct experience, books and similar media still serve a purpose by:

- extending direct experience beyond our own time into the past and the future, and beyond our own environment;
- replacing direct experience where, for example, direct experience might be harmful;
- structuring direct experience;
- preparing for direct experience; and
- projecting beyond direct experience into the worlds of abstraction, speculation, and fantasy.

Kinds of development

When we speak of 'the development of children' we are talking about a whole range of developments that sometimes take place together, sometimes have surges and periods of rest, and sometimes seem to be in competition for prominence.

The basic kinds of development may be listed as:

- physical
- intellectual
- language
- emotional
- personality
- social
- moral
- spiritual

As will be appreciated, this is a very artificial categorization, little more than a rather crude device to enable us to look at a complex matter. It is useful but it invites scepticism. It is doubtful if, in reality, one could

*'What is this wonderful book? Is it Aristotle? Pliny? Buffon? No; it is *Robinson Crusoe*' (*ibid*. p.147).

separate intellectual and linguistic development, or emotional and personality development, or moral and spiritual development. Perhaps it will have more meaning and be more acceptable when we consider the ways in which reading can support these various kinds of growth (see Chapter 3).

But first we need a map.

Theories of development

Considering how much attention has been given to 'child development' by psychologists and educationists, it should be possible to find a generally-accepted theory that will help us to order our thoughts. What we are looking for is a framework, an accommodating structure that will help us to organize our information and ideas. We need to have the basis for guidelines, not for a mechanistic procedure to match children with books.

The obvious basis for a theory would appear to be direct observation of actual children. By this method a sample of children of a certain age could be studied and, on the evidence collected, a profile of each age could be made. This approach was taken by a team of American researchers at the Yale Clinic of Child Development, led by Arnold Gesell in the 1930s and 1940s. Their findings were attractively presented in a succession of studies: *The first five years of life* (1940), *The child from five to ten* (1946), and *Youth: the years from ten to sixteen* (1956). In these studies, each age ('Eight years old', and so on) was systematically described in terms of typical behaviour: motor characteristics, personal hygiene, emotional expression, fears and dreams, self and sex, interpersonal relations, play and pastimes, school life, ethical sense, and philosophic outlook.

Scattered throughout these studies are useful indications of reading ability and reading tastes at particular moments of development. Thus, under 'Play and pastimes' in the section 'Five years old', in *The child from five to ten* (Gesell, *et al.*, 1946, p.73) we find:

> There is nothing a five-year-old likes better than being read to, although he may spend considerable time looking at books himself and may even pretend to read. He prefers stories about animals that act like human beings. He shows marked fondness for first-grade readers that tell about occurrences in the lives of children. A few FIVEs may like to listen to a reading of comic strips, regardless of whether they understand them.

Under 'Reading' in the section 'Eight years old' we have (*ibid*. p.181):

> Those EIGHTs who are just beginning to read well now enjoy reading spontaneously. Though EIGHT may read well, he may not spend as

16

much time at reading by himself as he did at seven and he again likes very much to be read to. He is beginning to enjoy hearing the classics of childhood. A modern favorite relates the wonderful, magical, and absurd adventures of Mary Poppins. EIGHT is also interested in books of travel, geography, and faraway times and places.

Comic books are still his favorites. This interest reaches a peak at eight and nine years. EIGHT buys, collects, barters, borrows, and hoards his comics. He is more likely to borrow than barter, since he does not want to part with his own. Though he still likes the animal and slapstick comics, he is branching out into the blood-and-thunder type.

What at first would appear to be an ideal set of models for those concerned with supporting children's reading is soon seen as being too 'pat'—too set in a particular culture and in a particular moment of time. It is all too bland, and the constant reference to the reader as 'he' is rather tiresome, implying as it does that there are no differences in the reading behaviour and tastes of boys and girls. There are also the foreseeable difficulties that emerge when one takes as the basis for study the concepts of 'normal' and 'typical' children. Who were these normal, typical children who provided Gesell and his co-workers with data? They were very small groups (some fifty or more 'subjects') from 'well-off', presumably campus, families. Viewed now, nearly half a century later, these studies—attractive though they are—seem remarkably dated, for children's rate of development has increased over the years and we are now more aware of the variety of kinds and degrees of development to be found among the individual boys and girls in one age group.

If we have to criticize the Gesell studies because they were too *unscientific*, we will have to criticize the monumental National Child Development Study because it is too *scientific*. Undertaken by the National Children's Bureau, this is a longitudinal study of breathtaking scale and thoroughness. Its sample was no less than every child born in England, Scotland, and Wales in one week in March 1958. The resulting publications, such as *From birth to seven* (1972), though far more systematic and scientifically cautious than the Gesell studies, make stark reading. There is much statistical evidence to support every finding about the effects of social class, social conditions, and schooling factors on reading performance, but there is little that provides useful insights.

Of far greater sociological value are the highly-readable studies by John and Elizabeth Newson. In *Four years old in an urban community* (1968) and *Seven years old in the home environment* (1976), we are given a detailed picture of the domestic background of a group of young readers and young non-readers, perhaps readers and non-readers in the making. There is a wealth of revealing evidence on the attitudes that affect reading: 'His daddy always takes him to bed, and he says "Can I have a story?" said an engineer's wife, "but he's been told now that he's getting a bit too old for stories"' ['He' is four] (Newson and Newson, 1968, p.274); '"Then I read her a story," said an actor's wife, "and Rupert listens, and then I show Rupert his little book"' [Rupert being sixteen months old] (*ibid.* p.275).

One would only wish to receive this kind of evidence with caution, hesitating to draw stereotypical impressions of the children of engineers and actors, and impressions gathered some decades ago, aware as we are that social behaviour and social attitudes change with the passing of time. Parental expectations, children's exposure to a range of experience, and the availability of structured education were different, for example, for the five-year-old in the 1930s and 1950s, and these are different from those of the late 1980s. The Newson studies do, however, suggest ways of looking at the backgrounds of those children we are setting out to serve.

If large-scale research has failed to provide the guidance we need, others have used direct experience and informed 'hunch' to give us help in serving a particular age group. Distinguished examples would include Nicholas Tucker, whose *The child and the book* (1981) is both theoretically sound and practically convincing, and the books of the New-Zealander, Dorothy Butler, *Babies need books* (1980) and *Five to eight* (1986). Dorothy Butler writes as a parent, grandparent, and believer in the value of reading. The books are practical, informal, and enthusiastic: one feels the presence in the author's life of real children as well as real books.

What are more rare and more revealing are studies of individual children's reading. Another New-Zealander, Dorothy White, provided one of the best examples with her *Books before five* (1954). This is the record of her daughter Carol's encounters with books. Carol is not, of course, a 'typical' child, nor is Dorothy a 'typical' mother, but the book has much to tell us about one child's perception of books and their contents. It has a particular value because the author provides the evidence and avoids indulging in theorizing and interpretation.

Dorothy Butler's study of her granddaughter, *Cushla and her books* (1979), is particularly valuable, since it chronicles the effects of lovingly-chosen books on a heavily-handicapped little girl.

Donald Fry, in his study, *Children talk about books: seeing themselves as readers* (1985), has shown what can be done if one is not daunted by the 'unscientific' nature of small samples, limited 'controls', speculation, and subjectivity. Fry is sensitive to his young readers (four girls and two boys), respects them, their opinions, and their privacy. The result, in contrast to more scientific surveys and experimentation, is illuminating and should encourage further investigations of a similar kind.

We are still in need of a theoretical basis or framework. Perhaps we will find it in the highly-influential work of the Swiss thinker, Jean Piaget.

Jean Piaget (1896–1980)*

One has to call Piaget a 'thinker' because he cannot be categorized as an educationist or a psychologist. (He is more accurately described as an epistemologist.) His interest concentrated on the intellectual development of children—on how they find the means of processing all the information they receive by their senses. He has also investigated the moral and play behaviours of children.

At the centre of Piaget's theory lie a number of basic concepts that owe a great deal to his interest in biology. *Schemata* (the singular form is *schema*) are short sequences of behaviour, sequences of activities by which the baby explores its environment, and sequences of reasoning activities in those who are older. Repertoires of schemata are built up as an organism adapts to its environment. Piaget identifies two fundamental aspects or modes of adaptation: *accommodation* and *assimilation*. Accommodation takes place when the organism alters, or accommodates itself, to outside reality: 'Accommodation is concerned with mastery of the environment through self-modifying aspects of behavior that bends the self to fit reality' (Levy, 1978, p.110). Assimilation is a more basic, primitive form of adaptation—virtual non-adaptation in which 'the individual bends the external environment to fit its currently existing cognitive level' (*ibid.* p.110). Young children's *egocentric* behaviour is assimilation since they are incapable of seeing anything except from their own point of view. Play behaviour, as we will see, is largely assimilation: the person playing decides that a piece of stick is a car or a gun and treats it as such until the play ends.

Piaget identified a number of stages in the development of children's reasoning powers. The most basic was in the period up to the age of about two years, the sensori-motor stage, when the world is explored physically—all that waving of arms and legs, sucking, and (later) crawling. A problem (finding food, making an interesting noise, making a friendly face appear) is solved by schemata of physical activity. The next stage, from about two to four years, Piaget calls the preconceptual stage. Here there is a degree of internalizing, of solving problems without physical activity, but children still have little equipment for reasoning. In the period

*For suggested further reading on Piaget, see Piaget (1926), Flavell (1963), and Boden (1979).

from about four to seven years, still a preconceptual stage, children still make judgements based on appearance rather than reason. They are unable to manipulate two elements at once (length and breadth, for example), they cannot perceive conservation (of weight or volume or mass), and are unable mentally to reverse processes. The evidence here is provided by the well-known experiments, now questioned, where children were faced with two identical tumblers of water, one poured into a wide, shallow container, the other into a tall, narrow container. Which holds the greater amount of liquid? Another experiment involved two sets of six sweets. One set is kept in a tight group, the other is spread out to make a large group. Which contains the greater number of sweets?

For older children—from, say, the age of seven years—now in the operational stage, some degree of reasoning is possible, usually based on observed evidence. The experiments that were set the 'preconceptual' children would offer no problems to the children at this stage, but they still cannot engage in abstract thinking. It is in the next stage, from the age of about twelve years, that children develop the skills of formal thought and logical reasoning.

It is not a simple matter to apply Piaget's ideas to reading. What Piaget has done is to remind us that children operate mentally in a way different from adults. This should cause us to be cautious when we make assumptions about what children have gained from a story. Carol White, at the age of three and faced with the escape of the Flopsy Bunnies, said: '''Poor Mr McGregor, he won't have any dinner.'' She did not see that if he had had rabbit for dinner it would be a case of ''Poor Flopsy Bunnies''' (White, 1954, p.35).

Piaget was not the first to draw our attention to the fact that children's behaviour is different from mature adult behaviour. Rousseau (1762, p.54) wrote in *Émile*: 'Childhood has its own ways of seeing, thinking and feeling; nothing is more foolish than to try and substitute our ways'. It is worth noting, as an aside, that though this may seem obvious, one has only to observe parents with children, or to catch oneself as a parent saying 'Don't be so childish!' to one's three-year-old, to realize that the reminder remains necessary.

Piaget, then, provided a way of investigating children's mental behaviour by looking at the talk and actions of real children, initially his own— Jacqueline, Laurent, and Lucienne—and also a theoretical basis for such study. He does not give us *simple* explanations but he does give us useful ones. If his methodology and his findings have been questioned by some (for example, Donaldson, 1978) this does not reduce our debt to him.

Piaget investigated the intellectual development of children, but Sigmund

Freud had already proved a means of exploring their emotional development.

Sigmund Freud (1856–1939)*

It is fashionable to criticize the work of Freud and his followers, and some of the criticism is justified, particularly that concerning his male-dominated viewpoint. The fact remains, however, that Freudianism (psychoanalysis) is still discussed and is still influential.

. What Freud provides is a workable and, on the whole, convincing hypothesis or model that enables us at least to describe, if not to explain, the workings of the mind—that is, people's behaviour and people's creations, such as visual art and literature. It also provides a clinical procedure for treating some psychological conditions, but this takes us beyond the scope of the present book.

So much of our behaviour is irrational, and not only our unpleasant behaviour. We are aware sometimes of the strength of unconscious activity. It shows itself in powerful emotions that surprise us, in the richness of dream images, and in phobias and prejudices. Freud acknowledges the unconscious and provides a means of exploring it and of living with it.

There is a problem in discussing Freud's ideas and in trying to apply them, as will soon become apparent. Any simplification of Freud's ideas, especially that of the 'Freud reduces everything to sex' order, grossly distorts those ideas and limits their usefulness. Having said that, we can cautiously attempt a summary of his main ideas.

At the heart of Freud's thinking is his model of the human mind (not the brain) consisting of three elements: the id, the ego, and the super-ego. The id is the centre of primitive desires and is at its most powerful, indeed it is extremely powerful, in the first months of life. At this stage it operates largely in the unconscious but it is soon partly modified by exposure to reality, that part becoming the ego. It is later further modified by that element of the mind that exerts a kind of moral judgement on what we do and think, the super-ego. There is often conflict between the unrefined, basic desires of the id, the more reasoned operation of the ego, and the idealism of the super-ego. The idea of the super-ego seems to encompass the Christian concept of the conscience, and describes those moments when we feel restrained in our actions ('I am letting myself down' or 'I am letting my ideal person down' kinds of feelings).

*For suggested further reading on Freud, see Stafford-Clark (1967), Wollheim (1973), and Freud (1986). Among his followers, the work on the emotional development of children by Anna Freud (1966), Klein (1986) and Winnicott (1964) is also notable.

More than this, Freud has provided an account of the human psyche's stages of development. These stages can be seen as centres of psychic concentration, phases of emphasis that, in 'normal' development, are passed through as we progress to being mature, integrated people.

Freud's phases are first the oral, up to the age of about one-and-a-half years when all activity is concentrated on the mouth, on sucking, and on taking in to oneself. It is followed by the anal stage, made popular by reference to 'potty-training'. It is the stage (going on until about the age of four years) that is dominated by the control of the bladder and bowels. It is the stage of conflict with parents, the stage when power is gained to give or to retain. Towards the end of this stage the phallic phase is entered. It is this period of development's description, with the discussion of Oedipal feelings and conflicts, that reveals Freud's male-dominated thinking. In this period the child reaches a stage of sexuality that gradually finds the opposite-sex parent attractive and the same-sex parent as a sort of rival for the attention and affection of the other-sex parent. It is also in this period (roughly from the age of three to six years) when sexual identity is established—usually with the same-sex parent providing the role model. There follows a period of latency, perhaps because development is centred elsewhere physically or intellectually, which is in turn followed by the genital phase—puberty, from which the person emerges as a mature, secure, integrated individual; or not.

This progression is not always smooth and trouble free. If an individual has problems at a particular stage he or she tends to regress to an earlier stage and to be dominated, or fixated, by the behaviour and attitudes of that stage. Thus adult people may be dominantly oral types, taking everything to them (engulfers) or gift-givers or miserly people of the anal type.

This is a gross simplification of a complex and largely convincing set of theories. Freud and his followers—and his former followers—described a number of mechanisms by which people protect or distort themselves, mechanisms such as repression, sublimation, projection, and so on.

As noted earlier, these theories have not only been applied to people but also to people's creations, such as works of art and writings. We are thus given a means of exploring some of the behaviour (especially the 'irrational' behaviour) of our users, of exploring stories some of which cry out for psychoanalytic examination (particularly 'classics' such as Lewis Carroll's Alice stories and J. M. Barrie's disturbing *Peter Pan*), and of understanding the profound impact of such books as those of Maurice Sendak. In their study, *Narratives of love and loss*, Margaret and Michael Rustin (1987) have applied a psychoanalytical approach to the examination of a group of modern children's novels and stories.

Norman N. Holland has, in his book, *The dynamics of literary response* (1975), provided a detailed account of the application of psychoanalytic theories to literature. He gives examples of oral books, but misses Norman Lindsay's *The magic pudding*, and anal books (all those miser stories, and comic obsession with slime and mud), characterizing *Through the looking glass* as a phallic fantasy, and so on. Most of his examples are from adult reading but the basis of his theory of literature, as is shown in Chapter 1, is childhood fantasies.

Long-surviving tales and rhymes, such as folk-tales and nursery rhymes, provide some of the readiest material for psychoanalytic examination. Perhaps they have survived because they contain topics and behaviour that deeply engage the unconscious. Bruno Bettelheim (1976)—not without his critics, see, for example, Tucker (1984)—clearly takes this view, for he has provided us with a detailed study of fairy tales, *The uses of enchantment*. It is worth stressing that this study did not arise out of a leisured academic interest but out of an urgent need for material to use therapeutically with highly-disturbed young people.

In Bettelheim's search for material that would give 'access to deeper meaning' (1976, p.4) he found currently-available children's books (in the 1970s) superficial: 'most of these books are so shallow in substance that little of significance can be gained from them' (*ibid*. p.4). In contrast, fairy stories dealt with 'universal human problems' and, more importantly, acknowledged that humans are often aggressive, selfish, irrational, anxious, and mortal. Where modern stories tended to present the ideal of human behaviour, the fairy story presents people as they are, the human situation as it is. It does not avoid the harsh realities:

> in fairy tales evil is as omnipresent as virtue . . . . Psychoanalysis was created to enable man to accept the problematic nature of life without being defeated by it, or giving in to escapism . . . . This is exactly the message that fairy tales get across to the child in manifold form: that a struggle against severe difficulties in life in unavoidable, is an intrinsic part of human existence—but that if one does not shy away, but steadfastly meets unexpected and often unjust hardships, one masters all obstacles and at the end emerges victorious.   (*Ibid*. p.8)

Bettelheim, while discussing the 'universal' and the personal significance of a range of traditional stories, provides convincing illustration of the power of reading to support self-exploration and self-integration. The therapeutic role of reading is discussed further in Chapter 6.

There is one further set of theories that may provide a structure for the study of reading behaviour: the theories of *play*.

The relevance of play*

We usually engage in an activity with a goal in mind; we undertake the activity with an aim. Reading is not always, perhaps not usually, such an activity. We often read without conscious purpose. The rewards are confidently expected, otherwise we would abandon reading and do something else, but the rewards are unanalysed, unformulated, unexpressed, and perhaps often unexpressable.

There is another set of behaviours that has this characteristic and that has received far more attention. It takes a variety of forms and has long bewildered scientists and philosophers because it appears to lack biological purpose. This set of behaviours is known as play.

Play is usually defined as any activity engaged in for the enjoyment it gives without any consideration of the end result. It is entered into voluntarily and is lacking in external force or compulsion. Play activity is characterized by joy, by lack of specific aim, and by being governed—if at all—by temporary and not 'universal' rules or regulations. Play is spontaneous and begins and ends informally. Once play activity becomes formalized, directed, structured by rules, and it takes place in a defined space ('field of play'), it moves into the related but distinct area of *games*. Play, in Piaget's terms, is largely assimilation; games are accommodation.

One view of play (this spontaneous activity found in the immature animal and in most humans of any age) is that it prepares the organism to meet and to cope with a wide range of situations. Primitive, limited creatures that can survive on a small repertoire of set-behaviour schemata do not play in infancy. Creatures that have to hunt, stalk, and capture difficult prey, spend long periods in play.

The writer's kitten is spending a lot of time, and not a little of his owner's patience, in developing a set of skills specifically to enable him to find and to cope with living prey. He does not seem to need to practise these skills. From the beginning he had dexterity and deadly accuracy, but he is being prepared for prey that also has dexterity and that may damage him if his approach is clumsy. Even though he appears to have been born with the skills, he needs to build up a substantial repertoire of techniques. Play, according to Jerome S. Bruner (1976, p.20) is 'the vehicle of improvisation and combination'. For many animals that means survival.

The human being (a far more complex creature inhabiting a far more complex world) needs to be highly adaptive and has a long period of play

*For suggested further reading on play, see Bruner, Jolly, and Sylva (1976) and Garve (1977).

in which to build up a vast repertoire of behaviours. Early play, with materials like sand, water, and clay, enables exploration of the material world. Play soon involves such 'materials' as language and ideas.

Play is a free, wide-ranging experimentation that has a part to play in relationships, in creative activity, and in scientific and technological advancement. In James Watson's account (1970) of the discovery of the structure of DNA—where the non-scientist expects to find strictly-controlled and logically-sequenced reasoning—there is an element of play: 'All we had to do was to construct a set of molecular models and begin to play' (*ibid*. p.48); 'R. D. B. Fraser . . . had been doing some serious playing with three-chain models' (*ibid*. p.133). (Apart from the specific use of the word 'play' by Watson, much of the investigation seems to have been undertaken in the spirit of play.)

This is not a total misuse of the word but an attempt to describe the process where a wide range of possibilities, some wilder than others, some orthodox some not, are considered. This process is characterized by its freedom, informality, and range. Here we are not in the realm of childhood behaviour but we are in the realm of play.

One form of play that is particularly important in the development of children explores human roles. In playing mothers and fathers, hospitals, and school, children are not only finding out what people *do* but also how they *feel*. In caring for a doll or in constructing conversations between soft toys or puppets, children explore how it feels to be a parent rather than a child, a nurse rather than a patient, a teacher rather than a pupil. More than this, such play provides insights into how people interact—arguing and fighting, loving, working together, playing together, sharing.

Of course, stories and information books also provide similar insights into what people do and their feelings. Perhaps more importantly they provide play material: ideas, content, and stimulus for play.

When play is concerned with the exploration of ideas and language, then reading (particularly the reading of stories and poetry) has a further contribution to make. Nonsense provides a particularly interesting case, especially that of Lewis Carroll (1865, p.77), for it is not merely the absence of sense but a means of playing with logic:

> The executioner's argument was, that you couldn't cut off a head unless there was a body to cut it off from . . . . The King's argument was that anything that had a head could be beheaded, and that you weren't to talk nonsense. The Queen's argument was that, if something wasn't done about it in less than no time, she'd have everybody executed, all round.

Play and reading are concerned with exploring; exploring the 'real', the immediate world and the world of speculation, the world of 'what if . . . ?' Play and reading are concerned with preparation, with providing the means of dealing with the problems and opportunities of human life.

To summarize this section we will consider the work of Jerome S. Bruner and his colleagues. They have done as much as anyone to establish the biological functioning of play. They have identified (Bruner, Jolly, and Sylva, 1976, p.15) the basic function of play as 'the opportunity for assembling and reassembling behaviour sequences for skilled action'. In human play there is concentration on preparation for social life through symbolic play, that is play where there is a breaking down of the limiting distinction between the real and the imagined. Play can be a testing-out of behaviour (aggressive and sexual behaviour, for example) in the safety of the play context. In Bruner's words, play 'is a means of minimizing the consequences of one's actions and of learning, therefore, in a less than risky situation . . . . [It is an] opportunity to try combinations of behaviour that would, under functional pressure, never be tried' (Bruner, 1976, p.38). Play may also serve 'the individual child in working through his own problems or fulfilling his wishes at the fantasy level' (*ibid.* p.49).

The reader will already be sensing the close relationship between play and story-making ('storying'), and between play and reading stories and poems. Indeed Bruner himself (1986), after studying cognitive thinking and play behaviour, has now become interested in narrative and the role of the reader.

Peter Hutchinson (1983, p.vi) has noted that 'the study of literary play deserves far more detailed attention than it has yet aroused' and has provided a useful introduction to the subject in *Games authors play* (*ibid.*). Despite the lack of studies, much of what follows in this book derives from the application of theories of play to the study of reading.

References and further reading

Bettelheim, Bruno (1976) *The uses of enchantment: the meaning and importance of fairy tales*, London: Thames & Hudson.

Boden, Maragaret A. (1979) *Piaget*, (*Fontana modern masters* series), London: Fontana. (This study takes into account all the aspects of Piaget's work and is far from a light read.)

Bruner, Jerome S. (1986) *Actual minds, possible worlds*, Cambridge, Mass.: Harvard University Press.

Bruner, Jerome S. (1976) 'Nature and uses of immaturity', in Jerome S. Bruner, Alison Jolly, and Kathy Sylva (eds.) *Play: its role in development and evolution*, Harmondsworth: Penguin, pp.28−64.

Bruner, Jerome S., Jolly, Alison, and Sylva, Kathy (eds.) (1976) *Play: its* role in development and evolution, Harmondsworth: Penguin. (A wide and interesting selection of papers.)

Butler, Dorothy (1979) *Cushla and her books*, Sevenoaks: Hodder & Stoughton.

Butler, Dorothy (1980) *Babies need books*, London: The Bodley Head.

Butler, Dorothy (1986) *Five to eight*, London: The Bodley Head.

Carroll, Lewis (1865 (1975)) *Alice's adventures in Wonderland*, London: Oxford University Press.

Davis, Madeleine, and Wallbridge, David (1983) *Boundary and space: an introduction to the work of D. W. Winnicott*, Harmondsworth: Penguin, rev.edn.

Donaldson, Margaret (1978) *Children's minds*, London: Fontana/Croom Helm. (Among other things, Donaldson questions Piaget's ideas about egocentrality and children's inability to reason deductively. Children may have communication problems with experimenters rather than a lack of reasoning ability.)

Flavell, John H. (1963) *The developmental psychology of Jean Piaget*, New York: Van Nostrand. (Though written with impressive clarity, this standard study is, due to its length, little less forbidding than Piaget himself. There are, however, a number of short introductions, written initially for teachers, which may be found useful.)

Freud, Anna (1966) *Normality and pathology in childhood: assessments of development*, London: Hogarth Press.

Freud, Sigmund (1986) *The essentials of psychoanalysis*, compiled by Anna Freud, Harmondsworth: Penguin. (Freud's own writings are highly readable and there is a substantial selection of them in this one-volume work compiled by his daughter. Although Freud had limited specific interest in children, some of his followers concentrated on the emotional development, and on 'normal' and 'abnormal' behaviour in young people. Notable examples are Anna Freud (1966), Melanie Klein (1986), and D. W. Winnicott (1964).

Fry, Donald (1985) *Children talk about books: seeing themselves as readers*, Milton Keynes: Open University Press.

Garve, Catherine (1977) *Play (The developing child* series), London: Fontana/Open Books. (A useful little introduction to play.)

Gesell, Arnold *et al.* (1940) *The first five years of life*, London: Methuen.

Gesell, Arnold *et al.* (1946) *The child from five to ten*, New York: Harper & Row.

Gesell, Arnold *et al.* (1956) *Youth: the years from ten to sixteen*, London: Hamish Hamilton.

Holland, Norman N. (1975) *The dynamics of literary response*, New York: W. W. Norton Library.

Hutchinson, Peter (1983) *Games authors play*, London: Methuen.

Klein, Melanie (1986) *The selected Melanie Klein*, edited by Juliet Mitchell, Harmondsworth: Penguin.

Levy, Joseph (1978) *Play behavior*, New York: John Wiley.

Morrish, Ivor (1967) *Disciplines of education*, London: Allen & Unwin.

National Children's Bureau (1972) *From birth to seven*, London: Longman/NCB.

Newson, John, and Newson, Elizabeth (1968) *Four years old in an urban community*, London: Routledge and Kegan Paul.

Newson, John, and Newson, Elizabeth (1976) *Seven years old in the home environment*, London: Routledge and Kegan Paul.

Piaget, Jean (1959) *The language and thought of the child*, 3rd edn, London: Routledge. (All Piaget's books, including this, his first, are difficult to read and to understand. See Flavell (1963), above, for the standard study.

Rousseau, Jean Jacques (1762 (1911)) *Émile*, London: Dent, Everyman's Library.

Rustin, Margaret, and Rustin, Michael (1987) *Narratives of love and loss: studies in modern children's fiction*, London: Verso.

Stafford-Clark, David (1967) *What Freud really said*, Harmondsworth: Penguin. (A sensible and accessible introduction to Freud.)

Tucker, Nicholas (1984) 'Dr Bettelheim and enchantment', *Signal*, no.43, pp.33−41.

Tucker, Nicholas (1981) *The child and the book*, Cambridge: Cambridge University Press.

Watson, James D. (1970) *The double helix: a personal account of the discovery of the structure of DNA*, Harmondsworth: Penguin.

White, Dorothy (1954) *Books before five*, London: Oxford University Press/New Zealand Council for Educational Research.

Winnicott, D. W. (1964) *The child, the family and the outside world*, Harmondsworth: Penguin. (An introduction to this, and Winnicott's other works, will be found in Davis and Wallbridge (1983).

Wollheim, Richard (1973) *Freud* (*Fontana modern masters* series), London: Fontana. (A sensible and accessible introduction to Freud.)

3

Reading and development

A wide range of influences supports the development of children. Initially the mother transmits messages about love and security, or anxiety and rejection, through her body. As children's worlds expand, the home—through the people, animals, and objects of which it is composed—provides educational opportunities. Later, play-group and school greatly extend the range of influences, especially through exposure to a wide range of planned and spontaneous social interactions with peers.

It is easy to exaggerate the contribution that the reading of books and other materials make to development if one ignores the rich experiences provided by home, school, and peer group, but reading enables (as can be seen from the discussion in earlier chapters) a complementing of direct experience, a further widening of children's worlds.

In order to look more closely at the assistance reading can give to growth—in both its cognitive (intellectual) and affective (emotional) aspects—we adopt the list of types of development mentioned in the last chapter.

Reading and physical development
It is clear that a baby or a young person is able to grow anatomically and physiologically without hearing stories or reading books. However, the latter have a part to play from the period of nursery rhymes and finger and other basic-activity games. There was a time when parents had a repertoire of such material 'in their heads', but the oral handing down seems to have failed for many people. The new parent is often unprepared and may need to turn to books for help with the words and games needed for those periods of child bouncing, rocking, and cuddling. The enjoyment of gross physical activity goes on for a long time, progressing to skipping and rushing-about games. As one performs 'Round and round the garden like a teddy bear' or 'To market, to market to buy a fat pig' for the hundredth time, one may conclude that the period of enjoyment is much longer for children than for adults.

Later rushing-about games may be more organized and contentful when children base their play on ideas from a shared story or group of stories heard, seen, or read. Some play-school and school activities are planned in this way, and many computer games require an intimate knowledge of *The hobbit* or some other well-known story.

Information books (written in a range of styles from the jolly to the earnest) provide explanations of how the body works, how it should be maintained, and how it may be developed. These become particularly important with the onset of puberty when the individual needs the support and reassurance of sound and sane information, and of novels that give honest accounts and insights into the emotional life of the adolescent—the 'how it feels'. Usually there is family and peer-group support at such times but the book provides a privacy, an intimacy, that seems appropriate at this particular period.

Thus, books (and such materials as instruction videos) continue through life to support physical development, latterly by helping in the improvement of sports and other leisure skills. There is no substitute for the guidance and direction of a good coach, but such people are not always available or affordable.

Reading and intellectual development

Much reading, perhaps most, is undertaken to obtain information, to learn more about our immediate environment and the wider environment: nature, space, the human environment, and so on. In the process we develop skills in dealing with a variety of intellectual strategies. Our first information books provide facts in direct narrative form—the life of the frog, what happens at airports, costume, and so on. Later information books use more complex means of examining and explaining, requiring an understanding of such structures of argument as cause-and-effect, comparison-and-contrast, analysis-and-synthesis, chronology, evolutionary development, general-to-specific, and specific-to-general. Hence some kinds of reading lead to more intellectually-demanding thought, challenging ideas, concepts and structures that build up the skills of critical observation, bodies of knowledge, and, at a further stage, wisdom.

It is worth noting at this point that many young readers do not recognize the distinction between 'fiction' and 'non-fiction' that many adults seem to find critically significant. For many young readers information books (or the best of them) are exciting, imaginative, and illuminating. In short, they possess qualities that some myopic adults would argue were the unique contribution of 'Literature'. Something of this deep attachment and influence can be seen in Edmund Gosse's (1949) life-long memories of reading the *Penny cyclopaedia*.

Through reading, direct experience can be extended through space and time. With regard to the gradual exploration of historical time, reading not only helps to develop the concept of periods of time and of progression (if not progress), but it also (through the historical novel) enables the reader to 'feel what it was like'. There is a certain dishonesty, or at least a limitation of truth, in presenting only historical facts. Figures about child labour in coal mines in the nineteenth century, or about evacuation of children in the Second World War, do not begin to give any impression of what it was like to work in a coal mine or to be evacuated. Part of the truth is withheld until the affective aspect of a historical situation is introduced.

The modern historical novel has been particularly successful in giving convincing pictures of moments of history as experienced by young women as well as 'plucky boys': Jill Paton Walsh's *A parcel of patterns*, Hester Burton's *Time of trial*, and K. M. Peyton's Flambards novels are examples and, as experienced by 'the lower orders', Barbara Willard's *Ned only* and K. M. Peyton's *The right-hand man*. Thus historical fiction, which once tended to concentrate on the grand thoughts and actions of grand people (sorts of super-persons), now provides the means of closer contact between the present-day reader and the past. Rosemary Sutcliff (1973, p.308) has stressed that 'history *is* people—and people not so very unlike ourselves'. At the same time concern for historical accuracy, as well as psychological honesty, is a characteristic of the modern writer.

There is yet another area of intellectual activity that is supported by reading, and this is speculation of the 'what if . . . ?' kind, found in science fiction (SF). Under the influence of Orwell and Aldous Huxley, SF for young people extends movements, ideologies, and trends of the present (technological advances and human organizational and philosophical developments) into a possible future. What tended in the past to be action stories have, without loss of excitement in the best examples such as the stories and novels of John Christopher and Nicholas Fisk, become serious exercises in prediction.

The processes of learning to read and reading with competence are concerned essentially with developing intellectual skills and abilities. They not only provide the matter for intellectual activity—facts, knowledge, range of probabilities, and so on—but they also have the quality of 'encouraging reflective thought and awareness of the processes of the mind' (Donaldson, 1978, p.106).

It would be difficult to read without questioning, without struggling to comprehend, without being stimulated to further thought, and without becoming aware of one's own mental processes.

Margaret Donaldson says (*ibid*. pp.94−5):

31

The child who is learning to read is in a situation that is likely to encourage him to begin to consider possibilities in relation to at least one important act of thought: the apprehension of meaning. As one child put it: 'You have to stop and think. It's difficult!' .... Those very features of the written word which encourage awareness of language may also encourage awareness of one's own thinking and be relevant to the development of intellectual self-control, with incalculable consequences for the development of kinds of thinking which are characteristic of logic, mathematics and the sciences.

Reading is, as is shown in Chapter 1, thinking under the stimulus of print and picture. It is difficult to conceive of such thinking taking place without the growth and development of intellectual ability. It does not end with childhood, of course, but is a life-long process.

Reading and language development

Reading is partly about the enjoyment of language, the exciting and illuminating use of one's own language by people who are proficient in the use of written language. In a similar way, sound cassettes, radio, cinema, visits to the theatre, story-telling sessions, poetry readings, and performances of vocal music provide the opportunity for the enjoyment of spoken and sung language.

Rhymesters, poets, writers, and jokers of all kinds—and their audiences—have always loved playing with words. It is the play of sound, rhythm, and sense, of enjoyment of competence, and of surprise:

Hey diddle diddle,
The cat and the fiddle,
The cow jumped over the moon;
The little dog laughed
To see such sport,
And the dish ran away with the spoon.

(Opie and Opie, 1951, p.203)

'Twas brillig and the slithy toves
Did gyre and gimble in the wabe:
All mimsy were the borogoves,
And the mome raths outgrabe.   (Carroll, 1865, p.134)

A musty, dusty leathery smell of boys, books and ink. Words drone and a family of flies stagger through the heavy air as if in pursuit of them. But they turn out to be of Ancient History, so the flies blunder moodily against the parlour window beyond which the June sun ripens tempting dinners at roadsides and down by the strong-smelling beach; day after day after day.   (Garfield, 1971, p.7)

32

Language is, as we see from the first example, an enjoyment that begins before speech (perhaps before birth) with rhythms and sounds. It is soon supported by words that a child can not only respond to but also make. One of Leila Berg's grandchildren, Martha, at the age of eighteen months had a speaking vocabulary of 258 words (Berg, 1977, pp.26−9) and no doubt a more extensive hearing vocabulary since she was a full member of the family's conversation group and stories were part of her life. Martha was building up a vast resource that was enabling her to ask and to tell, to hear and to enjoy.

At one time childhood reading was justified mainly in terms of vocabulary growth: reading increased vocabulary. This seems a weak argument much in the spirit of the Andy Capp cartoon which read (if memory serves):

'Why do you play football at your age, Andy?'
'It keeps me fit.'
'Fit for what?'
'More football!'

Language development is more important than vocabulary building and offering dauntingly-high standards of written and spoken language. It would be a pity if reading replaced talking and writing—that is the fate of the 'book-worm', the person who is happier and safer among books than among people. Language development is about improved thinking for greater grasp of the world, for exploring the world and enjoying the world. It is about improved expression of one's own and other peoples' ideas, and the communication of those ideas. It is about the enjoyment of language through speaking and joking and 'creative' writing: poetry, stories, diary-keeping, letter-writing. Reading has a part, but only a part, to play in that process.

Reading and emotional development

The Rustins have written (1987, p.2) that all the modern writers of fiction for children they examined 'are concerned, in one way or another, with issues of emotional development in children'. This is hardly surprising since one of the major activities of childhood is coming to terms with emotions, managing emotions, and establishing to what extent our own society, community, or family finds the display of emotions acceptable.

Exploring and experimenting with emotions (one's own and other people's) in real situations can be hazardous, and so play situations are often used as a sort of laboratory. In play—role-play with dolls or peers— one can explore feelings without taking risks, without having to face the consequences of one's behaviour. Thus play aggression, play sexuality,

33

or play challenging of conventions is acceptable where actual serious behaviour of these kinds would carry penalties. Humour has a similar function as any copy of *The Dandy* or *The Beano* will demonstrate. Much of the comic-strip material (violence, challenging of authority figures, the suggestions of sexual and scatological matters) would be anti-social behaviour outside the protective humorous framework.

Clearly much that is read provides insights into the emotional lives of others, and at the same time of ourselves. It helps the young reader to come to terms with his or her own non-rational, unconscious-dominated behaviour. If nothing else it shows that our own irrationality is shared by others.

Much that is read offers the opportunity to witness a range of emotions from a position of safety. Wolfgang Hildesheimer (1985, p.201), in his 'warts-and-all' study of Mozart, suggests that music offers similar opportunities: 'Why else should we need music but for its ability to satisfy our longing for emotional experience, without our having to undergo the deep tumult at its root'.

Much that is read, from nursery rhymes and fairy stories to the young adult novel, enables one to experience 'at one remove' a range of emotions. In reading, or being read to, one has the security of knowing that one has the ability to withdraw from the emotional situation as soon as one wishes or needs to do so. It is this choice that helps to make reading a pleasurable experience. Although tension may be built up, fictitious treatment usually involves the releasing of that tension (by the 'happy ending', for example) or the reader can terminate the situation by lifting his or her eyes from the page.

There is further protective distancing if the exploration of emotions is placed in a historical, fantasy, or SF framework. The embarrassments of first love and sexuality, and particularly the nature of violence and cruelty, become bearable or 'handlable' in a story set in the past. An example of treating violence would be the opening pages of *Horned helmet* by Henry Treece. The raw emotions depicted in such stories would be unbearable if they were within a contemporary setting: it is the thought that 'this happened in the past' that buffers the reader. Unfortunately, recent (and continuing) revelations of child abuse show that 'this' did not merely happen 'in the past'. Some children will be reading about something close to their own experience, close to their own emotional world.

Not only does a story or novel provide a safe distance from the experience but it also enables far deeper knowledge of people than is common in real life. We can know far more about a fictional character than we can about another human, even more than we can know about

ourselves. The Rustins (1987, p.15), no doubt taking up some ideas of
E. M. Forster's (see below), say:

> In the real world ... we have to rely on momentary impressions, third-party reports, interpretations of expressions and remarks, letters, faces in the crowd, inferences based on knowledge of our own feelings, to understand others. We may in fact know more and not less about a fictional character than about most real people of our acquaintance. This is why fiction, including children's fiction, is so irreplaceable a form of human knowledge.

Forster (1962, p.54) says: 'In daily life we never understand each other .... We know each other approximately, by external signs, and these serve well enough as a basis for society and even for intimacy. But people in a novel can be understood completely by the reader, if the novelist wishes; their inner as well as their outer life can be exposed'. He adds (*ibid*. p.70):

> When a character in a book is real: it is real when the novelist knows everything about it. He may not choose to tell us all he knows .... But he will give us the feeling that though the character has not been explained, it is explicable, and we get from this a reality of a kind we can never get in real life .... We cannot understand each other, except in a rough and ready way; we cannot reveal ourselves, even when we want to; what we call intimacy is only a makeshift; perfect knowledge is an illusion. But in the novel we can know people perfectly, and, apart from the general pleasure of reading, we can find here a compensation for their dimness in life.

In discussing the help that reading can provide in exploring and explaining emotional lives, one comes upon a clue to the disappointment that is sometimes felt with writers as diverse as Arthur Ransome and Enid Blyton. Their characters do not seem to lead full, emotional lives.

Arthur Ransome's children are so sensible, responsible, and restrained. Their affection for each other and for their hero father is restrained. Even their fantasizing is restrained:

> 'It's a queer sort of crossing of Greenland ... coming back with a sick sheep.'
> 'Count it a Polar bear,' said Titty.   (Ransome, 1933, p.143)

They do occasionally emit a mild 'By Jove' or 'Bother everything' but their emotional range bears little comparison with that of most children. This 'taboo on emotions' is in sharp contrast to the open expression of emotion in earlier stories. Frederic W. Farrar's *Eric, or, little by little* of 1858 is the often-quoted example, in which the boys show open affection for each other in a way that would be at least ridiculed in our own harsh world of emotional constraint:

> In an instant they were kneeling in silence by the bed with bowed foreheads; and the sick boy tenderly put his hands on their heads, and pushed the frail white fingers through their hair, and looked at them tearfully without a word, till they hid their faces with their hands, and broke into deep suppressed sobs of compassion.
>
> 'Oh hush, hush!' he said, as he felt their tears dropping on his hands while they kissed them; 'dear Eric, dear Monty, why should you cry for me? I am very happy.'   (Farrar, 1858, p.135)

> 'Oh, how very beautiful these primroses are! Thank you, thank you, for bringing them . . . I will keep them, for your sake, Eric, till I die . . . *you* Eric, who I love best in the world.'   (*Ibid*. p.137)

Farrar's sentimentality may be excessive but we may envy his freedom to recognize and express childhood affection as well as childhood aggression ('"I'll kill you for that," said Barker, leaping at Eric, and seizing him by the hair' (*ibid*. p.73). Farrar was free of two taboos of our own time: the taboo on affection and the taboo on the dicussion of death.

Enid Blyton's characters do show emotions—they show affection and they get angry—but they are obvious and unrevealing, the writer judging that this shallowness is appropriate for young readers. Food is often the stimulus for feelings of enthusiasm and, one suspects, of affection:

> Janet . . . came running in, flung her arms round Cookie and gave her a smacking kiss.
>
> 'What's for dinner?' she said.   (Blyton, 1962, p.8)

> 'Janet, look—dozens and dozens of chocolate biscuits of all kinds! Gosh! . . . Oh, Auntie Lou, you *are* generous! Are they really all for us?'   (*Ibid*. p.9)

Even the adult characters tend to exhibit undeveloped, immature emotions: '"Women are always soft and silly," said her husband in a tone of great disgust. "It's a good thing *you* don't know any secrets— you'd give them away to the milkman!"' (Blyton, 1955, p.24). The young reader is not likely to gain much insight into mature emotional behaviour or into depths of feeling and their expression from reading Enid Blyton's stories. In *Look out Secret Seven*, the old General cries over the loss of his medals and the children are angry about the stealing of birds' eggs. In *Five go to Mystery Moor*, George ('Georgina by rights' says the explanatory blurb) has the bitter experience of jealousy when the group is joined by 'another girl ... who would rather be a boy, and tries to act like one!'—Henry (Henrietta 'by rights'). There is an opportunity to explore these feelings but the reader is rushed along and such matters are not allowed to interrupt the flow of the story.

J. M. Barrie's *Peter Pan* presents a special case. Some young readers find it disturbing, not because the characters lack emotion but because the whole story expresses emotional immaturity or instability. Barrie is ambivalent (at best) about 'growing up'. The story is 'an insecure read' for young people who share that ambiguity and seek reassurance.

Reading and personality development

Much reading, as we have seen and as is further discussed in the next sections, is concerned with exploring other people's attitudes and behaviour. Much reading is also concerned with ourselves, our inner selves, our own identity. Lewis Carroll's Alice spent much of her time, in the perplexity of early puberty, trying to find out who she was: '"Who in the world am I?" Ah, *that's* the great puzzle!?' (Carroll, 1865, p.18). The search for self is life long: finding out one's unique tastes, interests, beliefs, values, opinions, commitments, career, abilities, strengths, shortcomings, and failures—one's conscious and unconscious being.

Marcel Proust (1983, p.949) would say that reading is one of the means of self-discovery: 'In reality every reader is, while reading, the reader of his own self. The writer's work is merely a kind of optical instrument which he offers to the reader to enable him to discern what, without this book, he would perhaps never have perceived in himself'.

Not only novels and stories but also information books, biographies, poems and plays, and films and TV programmes that explore emotionally and intellectually personality and social life contribute to this process of self-exploration.

Exposure to a large collection of information books enables children to discover their own interests; in many cases 'passions' would be a more accurate description. Early introduction to animal books, or ballet books or ancient history, may be the beginning of a life-long hobby or career. (The present writer's introduction to Wallis Budge's books on ancient Egypt, long before he could read them with understanding, led him—forty years later—to the temples of Karnak and Luxor and to the Valley of the Kings.)

Other reading can assist with self-identity in terms of our sexual identity, our ethnic and cultural and geographical identity, and our religious and moral selves. Many of these matters are areas of conflict: conflict with parents, friends, school, or our inner selves. Reading can sometimes provide guidance and support, especially in showing that others have had similar confusions and conflicts, and have survived.

Reading and social development

The great human art is to live (in a range of relationships and degrees of harmony and understanding) with fellow humans while retaining one's own individuality. Such are the complexities of these relationships and the means of establishing and sustaining them, that they are the subject-matter of most stories and novels from Pooh to Proust.

Among the earliest stories children hear are those in which groups of creatures live together and put relationships to the test. Peter defies Mrs Rabbit's authority and experience as a mother by disobedience (in *The tale of Peter Rabbit*). Tigger tries the patience of his fellows not by wickedness but by excessive high-spirits; Rabbit attempts to teach Tigger a lesson in a rather unkind way (in Chapter VII, 'In which Tigger is unbounced', *The house at Pooh Corner*). Tove Jansson's inhabitants of Moomin Valley (1961, p.115) learn to live together in an atmosphere of Scandinavian hospitality:

> 'Oh!' said Moominmamma with a start, 'I believe those were mice disappearing into the cellar. Sniff, run down with a little milk for them.' Then she caught sight of the suitcase which stood by the steps. 'Luggage, too,' thought Moominmamma. 'Dear me—then they've come to stay.' And she went off to look for Moominpappa to ask him to put up two more beds—very, very small ones.

Moomintroll and the Snork Maiden feel the first flutterings of love and, for once, we are offered a complete family (the Victorian habit of removing one, or both, parents was a convention that survived into Ransome's time). While Tove Jansson's world is founded on family and guests, many stories, particularly older ones, centre on same-sex relationships: *The wind in the willows*, Norman Lindsay's *The magic pudding*, and Richmal Crompton's William Brown stories are concerned with groups of males (indeed *The wind in the willows* has a sort of gentlemen's club atmosphere). School stories are usually based on one-sex schools. Same-sex relationships have similar pressures and problems (and rewards, of course) as other relationships, and these stories seem particularly enjoyable and useful in periods when young people find the other sex 'silly', 'horrid', or worse.

Particular difficulties arise, perhaps, in establishing relationships with those who are smaller and less powerful and, possibly, to some extent dependent. One thinks of younger siblings and playmates, handicapped friends, and animals. Stories concerned with children and miniature people (Mary Norton's Borrowers stories, Pauline Clarke's *The twelve and the*

38

genii, and T. H. White's *Mistress Masham's repose*, for example) deal with these issues in a vivid, easy, and entertaining way. In these stories the young characters learn that their greater physical power does not give them the right to treat the little people as playthings or inferiors.

In Pauline Clarke's story, eight-year-old Max discovers the wooden toy-soldiers that had belonged to the Brontë children. Under his sympathetic eye they reveal that they are alive. Max has to establish a relationship with the soldiers: 'He had quite early realised that part of their life depended on their being left to do things by themselves and not being interfered with. He could oversee and suggest, but not dictate' (Clarke, 1962, p.160).

In T. H. White's book, ten-year-old Maria has to learn similar lessons when she discovers a group of Lilliputians. (She also learns to cope with tyrants—Mr Hater, the Vicar, and Miss Brown, the Governess.) These are the lessons all children have to learn, children in less exotic situations than Max and Maria. Lessons parents, teachers, and other adults have also on occasion to relearn.

Reading and moral development

Much of the content of social development is concerned with ethics. We have spoken, for example, of the responsibilities that go with relationships, such as daughter or son, sister or brother, trusted ('best') friend, lover, wife, husband, and so on.

In the past children's reading was seen to have the heavy purpose of providing the young reader with moral guidance, indeed moral direction. As Geoffrey Trease (1964, p.3) has said: 'For the first . . . two centuries [of children's literature] the terrible twins, Morality and Instruction, stalk arrogantly through almost every story'.

Even the light-hearted efforts of John Newbery did not break this emphasis. Cornelia Meigs (1969, p.66) has to call the period after Newbery (the period dominated by such purposeful writers as Sarah Fielding, Mrs Barbauld, Mrs Trimmer, and Hannah More) 'The Age of Admonition'. And the applied ridicule of Lewis Carroll (1865, p.81) took time to take effect:

' . . . and the moral of that [said the Duchess] is—"Be what you would seem to be"—or, if you'd like it put more simply—"Never imagine yourself not to be otherwise than what it might appear to others that what you were or might have been was not otherwise than what you had been would have appeared to them to be otherwise."'

It took a long time to break away from the idea that children were at best potentially evil and indolent, that they were little pitchers that had to be filled with information and moral guidance before they filled themselves with wickedness, idleness, and nonsense. John Rowe Townsend comments (1967, p.159) that 'simply giving children pleasure seemed too frivolous an aim to most nineteenth-century writers'. Not merely frivolous but indefensibly irresponsible.

That it was done so artlessly in the past, of course, does not mean that ideas of what is right and wrong should not be dealt with in stories and novels for young people. Indeed, it is difficult to think of the expression of any ideas that does not reveal a moral attitude. Modern writers do not over-stress a moral view but have sufficient faith in it to allow it to emerge, much as it does in everyday life. Of 'good children's books', Lillian Smith (1953, p.16) has said, 'Their values are sound and directly put. Yet they do not preach these principles, rather are they implicit in the writing'.

In 1967 John Rowe Townsend felt it necessary to draw attention to the return of heavy-handed didacticism in children's books, and critical evaluations of them. 'Years ago we threw the old didacticism (dowdy morality) out of the window; it has come back in at the door wearing modern dress (smart values) and we do not even recognize it' (p.159). Certainly there was much concern about 'right values' at that time and the writer can remember an American teacher asking Townsend himself at a conference if he was 'completely happy' about the 'irregularities' in the family of his *Gumble's yard*. (In this story of slum life, the children's father, the weak Walter, is not married to his companion, the fag-smoking Doris.)

The idea that stories should always show the ideal would soon, one feels, convince young readers that literature is not about life, or about any life the reader knows. And whose ideal are we being offered?

> Aunt Elena and Uncle Hal aren't our real aunt and uncle, but we love them as though they were. Aunt Elena was Mother's room-mate at school in Switzerland and they've been best friends ever since. Aunt Elena is a concert pianist, and she plays all over the country and in Europe, too. Uncle Hal, her husband, is a jet pilot.
>
> (L'Engle, 1966, p.13)

Here, in Madeleine L'Engle's *Meet the Austins*, worldly success is made some sort of virtue, as it is in her *A wrinkle in time* (1963, p.30): 'You've met my mother, haven't you? You can't accuse her of not facing facts, can you? She's a scientist. She has doctors' degrees in both biology and bacteriology.' And in her *A swiftly tilting planet* (1978, p.4):

> It was good to be home for Thanksgiving .... The twins, Sandy and Dennys, home from law and medical schools, were eager to hear about Calvin ... and the conference he was attending in London, where he

was ... giving a paper on the immunological system of chordates. 'It's a tremendous honour for him, isn't it, Sis?' Sandy asked. 'Enormous'.

One wonders what thoughts this invites in the minds of those young readers whose parents are 'mere' bus drivers, nurses, sheep farmers, or school teachers. Have their parents failed them? (See Townsend, 1971, pp.120—9, for an interesting assessment of Madeleine L'Engle.)

This smugness seems part of the moral message of Madeleine L'Engle's books, and the message is forced upon the reader. More recent writers have confidence in their role—as story-tellers rather than moral teachers— and more confidence in their young readers, most of whom have a working ethical sense. Thus a moral lesson can be given in a light-hearted manner:

'Learning? [says Meg the scullery maid] Give you a farthing for it! Mark my words, little one—a yewmanbeen's better off without it! What good's it ever done a soul? Brains? Wouldn't have 'em if you paid me! A penn'orth of heart's worth all your skinny clever heads! . . . . I saw some clever heads—once. When I was a little girl. Me mother— God rest her—showed me. Three of 'em: a Lord, a Sir and a Mister. On the Traitors' Gate. Cut off at the neck! Very clever heads, they was. And much good it did 'em! ''Meg!'' said she—and I'll always remember her words—''Meg! Take note. Heads without hearts is nought but bleeding pom-poms! Of no use to man, woman or child''.'

(Garfield, 1967, p.70)

It would be difficult for this important matter, the relationship between the intellect and human feelings, to be presented in any other way to young readers.

Important moral issues can be light-heartedly presented, as in Leon Garfield's *Smith* just illustrated, and as in Jeff Brown's *Flat Stanley* that deals unpretentiously with attitudes to people who are different, and with the nature of brotherly love. The moral itself can be something of a joke as in Russell Hoban's story (1974) where Tom, through his commitment to 'fooling around' thwarts Captain Najork and his hired sportsmen.

There are major moral issues of our time (famine, nuclear issues, conservation and pollution, freedom fighting and terrorism) that deeply involve and concern young people. Such issues are the subject of information books and works of fiction. The nuclear debate, for example, has been the subject of a picture book (Raymond Briggs' *When the wind blows*) and various novels such as Robert Swindells' *Brother in the land* and Louise Lawrence's *Children of the dust*. Information books, such as those in Franklin Watts' *Issues* series and Batsford's *Today's world* series, provide factual bases for discussion of world problems and opportunities.

Reading and spiritual development

One envies Saint Teresa of Avila (1957, pp.23−4), who appears to have had conviction and commitment almost from birth:

> We [Teresa and her brother Rodrigo] used to read the lives of the Saints together .... I used to discuss with my brother ways and means of becoming martyrs, and we agreed to go together to the land of the Moors, begging our way for the love of God, so that we might be beheaded there .... But having parents seemed to us a very great hindrance .... We decided to become hermits; and we used to try very hard to build hermits' cells in an orchard belonging to the house .... When I was with other girls I especially enjoyed playing at nunneries, and pretending to be nuns.

(Saint Teresa goes on to talk about the ill-effects of reading for amusement—specifically reading books of chivalry—but that does not invalidate this demonstration of the role of reading and play in childhood.)

For others spiritual direction has had to be hard won, a sifting of alternatives, a struggle with doubts and disappointments. For children in the late twentieth century there is the added difficulty that they do not live in a spiritually-secure environment, almost certainly lacking the supportive family and community that was Saint Teresa's world.

Although the present time could not be described as 'religious', there is a great interest in mythology, magic, the occult, eastern philosophies and religions, and the supernatural—everything, one is tempted to say, except a shared orthodoxy. To speak of a search for God or a relationship with God would perhaps be putting it too strongly. If nothing else, however, many people feel that the immediate, material world is not the only reality and they are searching, in a rather vague way, for 'The Other'. This latter reality, behind the 'surface' reality, is readily experienced, being entered when we are 'transported' by a particular musical experience, by a breath-taking piece of prose or poetry, or by just having an upsurge of feeling of being right with the world.

There is no shortage of books that show worlds behind the material one (the 'real' world), usually as the setting for a struggle between Good and Evil. Much traditional material—myths and legends, and fairy and folktales—deals with this conflict, as do such modern stories as John Masefield's *The midnight folk* and *The box of delights*, Susan Cooper's *The dark is rising* sequence, and Clare Cooper's books.

It is a sad fact of life that very few writers are capable of producing books that are both written from a position of commitment and are successful pieces of writing. 'The message' seems to overcome the elements of good story-telling. An exception, perhaps—though David Holbrook (1973), for one, would not agree—are the Narnia books of C.S. Lewis, but it might be argued that the story told allegorically in *The lion, the witch and the wardrobe* was told much more successfully in *The Bible*.

The 'young adult' novel

The first five years of life are a period of rapid development. The only other period of such rapid development is adolescence. The 'teens' are a period of profound changes: physiological, psychological, and social. They are a time of exploration, assertion, and challenge, and often of confusion, contradictions, and trauma.

It is not surprising, therefore, that a whole group of books have been written to serve the emerging adult by discussing adolescents' interests and problems in a fictional form. They are often cheap-looking paperback books, usually in series with names like *Sweet dreams*, *Teens*, *Couples*, and *Plus*. Most of them are directed at girl readers, the assumption seeming to be either that boys have no adolescent problems or that they read only 'action' books. Both assumptions should be questioned.

Adult critics tend to dismiss 'teenage' or 'young adult' novels as formula written—'romantic' rather than realistic, and routinely produced. A few writers (Betsy Byars, Joan Lingard, and Judy Blume, for example) are given critical attention, the rest are not.

If one suspends judgement and looks at a cross-section of these novels, one comes away quite impressed. The stories are brightly written, they deal with issues that really concern young adults, have convincing and positive heroines, and some of the authors have a gift for comedy. In short, although they are rarely 'literature', they are usually supportive of the emerging adult.

The stereotype is of stories exclusively concerned with drugs and unwanted pregnancies. In fact, a wide range of themes is tackled, some with impressive understanding and feeling. Such themes include expectations of life, employment and the problems of the first job, first love, relations with parents, divorced parents, step-parents, feelings of inadequacy, school and relationships with peers and teachers, and illness and grief.

It might be argued that there are works of literature that deal with these themes, and deal with them in a more thorough manner. The fact remains, however, that in the young adult novel we have a useful example of reading contributing to development: easily read, unpompous, and unauthoritarian, these books provide reassurance and role-models of the right kind.

As competent, adult readers we are sometimes aware that something we are reading is having a considerable effect upon us. We become conscious that a novel, a poem, a play, or a book concerned with science, religion, or whatever, is extending us. We are gaining greater knowledge, understanding, sensitivity, and appreciation. It is at such times, perhaps, that we wonder about the *unconscious* effect of what we read.

If this is something we experience as adults, how much more impact reading materials must have upon young readers—readers who are that much more receptive and who are at stages of rapid and profound development. It is for this reason that those concerned with young people—parents, teachers, librarians, and others—feel the need to provide a wide range of such materials as books, films, videos, and pictures, and to provide opportunities for acquiring the skills to obtain meaning from print and pictures.

References and further reading

Berg, Leila (1977) *Reading and loving*, London: Routledge & Kegan Paul.

Blyton, Enid (1955 (1969)) *Five have plenty of fun*, Sevenoaks: Knight Books.

Blyton, Enid (1962 (1973)) *Look out Secret Seven*, Sevenoaks: Knight Books.

Carroll, Lewis (1865 (1975)) *Alice's adventures in wonderland*, London: Oxford University Press.

Clarke, Pauline (1962) *The twelve and the genii*, London: Faber & Faber.

Donaldson, Margaret (1978) *Children's minds*, London: Fontana.

Farrar, Frederic W. (1858 (1971)) *Eric, or, little by little*, London: Hamish Hamilton.

Forster, E. M. (1962) *Aspects of the novel*, Harmondsworth: Penguin.

Garfield, Leon (1967) *Smith*, London: Longmans.

Garfield, Leon (1971) *The strange affair of Adelaide Harris*, London: Longman. (Opening lines.)

Gosse, Edmund (1949) *Father and son: a study of two temperaments*, Harmondsworth: Penguin.

Hildesheimer, Wolfgang (1985) *Mozart*, London: Dent.

Hoban, Russell (1974 (1978)) *How Tom beat Captain Najork and his hired sportsmen*, Harmondsworth: Puffin.

Holbrook, David (1973) 'The problem of C. S. Lewis', in *Children's literature in education*, no.10, pp.3–25.

Jansson, Tove (1961) *Finn Family Moomintroll*, Harmondsworth: Puffin.

L'Engle, Madeleine (1963 (1967)) *A wrinkle in time*, Harmondsworth: Puffin.

L'Engle, Madeleine (1966) *Meet the Austins*, London: Collins.

L'Engle, Madeleine (1978) *A swiftly tilting planet*, London: Souvenir Press.

Meigs, Cornelia (1969) *A critical history of children's literature*, New York: Macmillan, rev. edn.

Opie, Iona, and Opie, Peter (eds.) (1951) *The Oxford dictionary of nursery rhymes*, Oxford: Clarendon Press.

Proust, Marcel (1983) *Remembrance of things past*, Harmondsworth: Penguin, Vol.3.

Ransome, Arthur (1933 (1968)) *Winter holiday*, Harmondsworth: Puffin.

Rustin, Margaret, and Rustin, Michael (1987) *Narratives of love and loss: studies in modern children's fiction*, London: Verso.

Saint Teresa of Avila (1957) *The life . . . by herself*, Harmondsworth: Penguin.

Smith, Lillian (1953) *The unreluctant years: a critical approach to children's literature*, Chicago: American Library Association.

Sutcliff, Rosemary (1973) 'History is people' in Virginia Haviland (ed.) *Children and literature: views and reviews*, Glenview, Ill.: Scott, Foresman, pp.305−12.

Townsend, John Rowe (1967) 'Didacticism in modern dress', in *The horn book magazine*, Vol.43, no.2, 159−64.

Townsend, John Rowe (1971) *A sense of story: essays on contemporary writers for children*, London: Longmans.

Trease, Geoffrey (1964) *Tales out of school*, London: Heinemann, 2nd edn.

4

Learning to read

There is a considerable quantity of books, periodicals, and reports for
the teacher of reading. This chapter is intended for those who are not
teachers of reading but who, as parents, teachers, and librarians, wish
to support both the specialist teachers and the learner-readers.

Children are learning to read long before they have any formal reading
tuition. They become readers in the sense of having positive expectations
and motivation long before they go to school. They will need to develop
skills and to exercise skills to become competent, independent readers,
but they will be well on the road to enjoying reading.

We are, of course, presuming a great deal. We are thinking of the
advantaged children. We are thinking about those children who, whatever
their socio-economic background, have parents who have the time, or
somehow make the time, to talk with them, to read to them, to read for
themselves, and so to offer an example. These are parents who read for
their own pleasure and reward, and who wish their children to have
pleasure and reward too.

We need to support the children who, unless frustrated, are going to
find reading easy. We also need to support the less-advantaged young
people, those who have not been encouraged, by example or word, to
tackle what some (perhaps many) increasingly feel to be a very difficult
and unrewarding task. They start unmotivated and soon associate learning
to read with failure and frustration.

In order to help the learner-reader, particularly at the school stage, we
need to know how reading is 'taught'.

How is reading taught?
As we have said, many children are not taught to read. They have acquired
the ability to read much as they acquired the ability to speak, effortlessly,
'informally', and often unnoticed. Many parents are surprised to find their
young children reading, unaware that the skills have been picked up.

Thus the reading teacher is faced with groups of children at various
stages of motivation and preparation. Some can read a little. Some have

not begun to appreciate the purpose of print. The teacher will use a wide range of approaches and materials to bring them all up to an acceptable level of performance.

The famous Bullock report of 1975, *A language for life*, after an investigation of teaching in schools, came to the conclusion that 'there is no one method, medium, approach, device, or philosophy that holds the key to the process of learning to read' (DES, 1975, p.77). Most teachers would agree with this statement and, indeed, say that they use a variety of approaches and methods in their work, suiting them to the needs of the individual learner and the stage that pupil has reached.

The time-tested approaches are as follows:

1 *'Look-and-say'* This is a whole-word approach that requires the building up of a visually-recognized vocabulary. Most children enter school being able to read their own name and a few other words seen-and-said on television programmes, on labels on food, and on public notices. Big words like 'ambulance' and 'elephant' are easily learned as they have readily-recognized shapes.

2 *Phonic* In the phonic approach, words are built up from the sounds of the individual letters or groups of letters (phonemes such as *th*, *ph*, and so on). The English language presents difficulties if a purely phonic approach is attempted (silent letters in 'knife' and 'pneumatic', for example) but it is useful in dealing with the 'sounding out' of unfamiliar words.

3 *Whole sentence* In this approach (used when the learner dictates a caption for a drawing or painting—'Peter drew this picture' or 'Wendy and John are swimming in the sea'), the teacher writes the caption and the learner 'reads' it (in other words, repeats what the teacher reads). With this approach, *the language experience approach*, the learners' interest is held because they are using their own words and telling their own story.

4 *Psycholinguistic* The psycholinguistic or 'guessing-game' approach reflects the way that competent and learner-readers tackle a text in order to obtain meaning from it. This is reading using contextual 'cues', reading as problem-solving, 'playing for meaning', or 'having a stab at'.

As a competent reader you may find it difficult to read aloud. This is because you are not used to being shackled to the author's words. If you review what you have read silently, you may be surprised by the difference between what is on the page and what you have 'read'. The psycholinguistic approach takes this into account, but the teacher who is concerned with accurate decoding rather than—and not as well as—obtaining meaning will find 'mere guessing' unacceptable.

Modern approaches to supporting the learner-reader lay emphasis on an 'apprenticeship' approach where the learner is in partnership with a competent reader. This is the approach used throughout life to learn such important skills as speaking, food preparation, child care, and workplace activities. The competent reader can be an adult or another, more skilled, child. There is also a need for what might be called 'a competent listener—interested, patient, caring, and trusted—who may be a friendly ('special' is Leila Berg's—1977—word) adult, fellow child, teddy bear or family pet. Liz Waterland says (1985, p.42), 'My invitation . . . is "Come and read with me"'; 'I provide the lap, the text and the time; the learning is the child's' (*ibid.* p.45). (Note that Liz Waterland has modified her idea of apprenticeship since this 1985 pamphlet appeared: 'It seems to me now that the text, whether in print or in the child's own creation, is the guide and demonstrator, the adult and the child *together* are the apprentices—albeit at different stages of competence—who are feeling their way towards knowledge of the meaning of words' (Waterland, 1986, p.147).

The emphasis is on comprehension, obtaining meaning and pleasure, not on merely decoding skills. The skills used by competent readers—guessing, skipping, and skimming—are employed. Children are encouraged to tell and re-tell stories rather than read aloud.

Much of the success of an approach based on meaning and pleasure depends upon the quality of the reading materials. Reading schemes have been heavily criticized for a range of reasons. Bettelheim and Zelan (1982) found 'primers' to have little content, to be limited and repetitive: they gave the new reader little with which to engage. They were an insult to the learner-reader.

The following extract is from the opening pages of *With Peter and Susan*, the McKee Readers, book 3 (London: Nelson—no date, although from the illustrations it appears to be a pre-war reader. It was originally published by the American company Houghton Mifflin). It was withdrawn from a British primary school in 1987. It would not be difficult to find more recent examples:

See the ball go, Peter.
See it go.

Here it comes down, Peter.
See it come down.

The ball will not come down.
Do you see it, Peter?
I do.
I can see it.
It will not come down.

Can you see the ball, Peter?
Can you see it up there?

I can.
I can see where it is.
I will get the ball.
It is up there.

And so on. (Who are these strange people, Peter and Susan, who labour at the obvious? What kind of language is this? It is not a language the young reader—or indeed any reader—is familiar with. Is it a mad, mystical sort of poetry? And what is the story? How is the reader to become involved with the mysterious behaviour, the apparently motiveless behaviour, of the two characters?)

Much of Bettelheim and Zelan's 1982 study consists of criticism of primers. They are seen as exercises 'camouflaged as stories . . . and are accompanied by pictures depicting situations for the description of which the child knows he would use a wide vocabulary and a rather complex sentence structure' (p.221), a vocabulary and sentence structure very different from those used for the primer. 'The pretense that the constant repetition of a few words constitutes a story becomes an insult to the child's intelligence' (*ibid*, p.221).

Leila Berg (1977, p.49) has drawn attention to the sexual and social-class stereotyping and the absence of emotion in the stories:

> Although the family in the orthodox reader cannot exist at all—there is no family so griefless, angerless, humourless, or so utterly devoid of conflict as the family in the orthodox reader—it is recognisable in externals . . . the detached house . . . father at leisure with the lawn-mower (or going to the office with the brief case), the large dog and the aristocratic cat, the tidy organised family consisting only of one father, one mother, one son, one daughter.

(The writer's just-seven-year-old son has been reading *People we know*—level 6, book 1 in the Ginn Reading Programme—to him this morning, with evident enjoyment. The story was quite interesting, parts were amusing, but the main enjoyment was clearly in performance rather than matter. The achievement was to have finished another book rather than to have engaged with characters and plot.)

The solution for those taking the apprenticeship approach is to use *real* books instead of reading-scheme materials. Real books are those written by authors who have something they need to say and that have been published separately as children's books, not teaching aids. Real books are the books children encounter in story-telling sessions at home, in the library or play-group, and on children's television—books that become part of the reader's self, books to be remembered and revisited with anticipated pleasure.

A school reading programme*

The 'traditional' sequence of classroom activities concerned with the development of reading interests and skills probably begins with carefully-planned play activities. The talking that accompanies play with such materials as water, sand, clay, junk materials, and bricks, with dramatic role-play in the Wendy house and the model shop, and with imaginative play with miniature animals, people, and vehicles—all of this builds up spoken vocabulary. Objects in the classroom are soon labelled and a similar sight-vocabulary is built up ('shop', 'door', and, most importantly, the learner-reader's own name on peg, chair, and shelf).

There will be much looking at books to hunt for pictures to identify objects on the nature table and to help with model-making. The teacher will tell stories and read stories, building up vocabulary and, perhaps more importantly, show what rewards there are when one can read the print as well as the pictures. When watching the teacher read, some children will be learning how a book works—the left-to-right convention, for example, and how to turn the pages—for the first time. (Some children will find that English books work differently from those read in the mosque, synagogue, or at home.)

The learner's first reading will probably be from captions to paintings or drawings, captions written by the teacher using the words of the artist. This creation of reading material will continue throughout the primary school, with much individual work and group work, such as the class story, the class diary, the weather report, and so on. Much of this material, important to the group, will be read later to other children and to the teacher. As the time approaches to use published materials, reading schemes or carefully-selected 'real' books, there may be a preparatory

*Some of the material for this section was obtained from a well-structured Open University film. See Open University (1973) in 'References and further reading' at the end of this chapter.

period of sight-vocabulary building, using flash-cards (word-matching, word-reading, etc.).

Reading activities develop into individual reading sessions with the teacher, into private reading, and into reading for information (in order to understand something, to do something, or to write something). There will also be reading for personal pleasure and reading to share pleasure.

Among the great moments in the reading programme are those when writing has developed to the point where the learner-reader can read his or her own story to the teacher—a triumphant change of roles—and when children are found in quiet corners reading to each other. Reading has then become a voluntary activity associated with pleasure and achievement.

What the competent learner-reader brings to the task

The idea of 'reading readiness', a matter of much concern in the past, is now dismissed. Frank Smith (1985, pp.156−7) says:

> There is no intellectual or linguistic basis for the notion of readiness. If learning to read is regarded as a continual process of making more and more sense of written language, advancing with every reading experience and beginning with the first insight that print is meaningful, then it will be seen that there can never be anything specific for a child to be ready for . . . . When the use of the term 'reading readiness' in education is examined, it will be seen not to refer to readiness to read, nor even to readiness to learn to read, but to quite a different state of affairs, namely *readiness to cope with reading instruction.*

The learner who is well on the road to being a competent reader does bring a number of things to the task, a set of skills and attributes many of which are still developing.

He or she brings good sight and the beginnings of visual discrimination. The differences between *c*, *o*, and *e* are subtle, but they are significant in reading. Any adult who has been concerned with the design of type has re-experienced the need to see the importance of features (thin and thick strokes, serifs, and so on) of which they were previously unaware. There is a similar need for auditory discrimination since the differences between 'hat' and 'hut', and 'fin' and 'thin' are again subtle but significant. In the latter case there is the additional difficulty when children hear words pronounced in a way that disconnects them from the written form. The language of the playground, the street, and the home often bears little comparison with the language of books, even the language of the teacher. L. John Chapman (1987, p.9) says rather primly 'there are many that are proficient only in a non-standard version of English'.

The learner brings a rapidly-growing set of concepts, and a rapidly-growing spoken vocabulary to the task. These will have had a firm foundation in play and the talk that accompanies it, particularly if the learner has had the social and material opportunities provided by play-group or nursery school.

There is also the need for emotional stability. The disturbed, insecure, troubled youngster may have difficulties. Reading requires self-assurance, a certain amount of courage to 'have a go', and the ability to concentrate. The over-protected, the abused, the under-encouraged, and the forced may have difficulty in giving full attention, even in relaxing into the reading act. It needs to be said that some handicapped readers (brain-damaged or retarded) can fully enjoy books: we have the lesson of Cushla as an inspiration here (Butler, 1979).

The main thing the well-prepared learner brings to the task is positive expectations—expectations that reading will bring rewards of pleasure and understanding, and that he or she is going to learn to read and to enjoy the learning. The most difficult part of learning to read is learning that learning to read is worth the effort involved, and of being aware of the rewards of reading. Some children never learn that it is worth the effort and so do not learn to read efficiently. Some children who are able to read and have learned to read effortlessly are unaware of the rewards of reading and so do not read voluntarily.

As we have seen, current educational thinking tends to dismiss the idea of 'reading readiness', but there is a need to show children the benefits, the rewards, and the access reading gives to information, knowledge, and entertainment. This may or may not happen in the home through story-telling and observing others reading.

Supporting the learner-reader

Before considering direct assistance to the learner-readers themselves, there is another group who may need support—the parents. Most writers stress the importance of parental attitudes and parental activities. Margaret Meek (1982, p.26) says that 'The parents' role ... is to encourage the child to believe that reading is a worthwhile and pleasurable thing to do, that literacy is within his grasp, and to provide the means for his enjoyment and success'.

Bettelheim and Zelan (1982, p.54) stress that

It is not objective merit, but high parental valuation, that makes reading so attractive to the child. This appeal does not emanate from the rational and utilitarian purposes parents may satisfy through reading: rather, the child responds to the parents' emotional absorption in reading. What makes it attractive to him is that it seems to fascinate his parents. It is their secret knowledge that the child wants to be able to share. The more parental devotion to reading and the child's belief in its magic propensities coincide, the easier time a child will have in learning to read, and the more important and enjoyable reading will be to him.

So much is, perhaps, obvious. The fact remains, however, that many parents, especially first-time parents, although motivated to help their children, have no idea what to do. (This is written with sympathy. The author remembers the first time he was left with his first, brand-new child. What do you say to a baby? What tone of voice do you use? It was some time before the pleasurable realization occurred that real communication could take place, that noises, grimaces, and gestures could bridge the gap where there were no shared words and thus give mutual delight.)

First-time parents may not know how to tell stories or share pictures; they may not know what books are available or how they should be used; and they may not realize how important and how enjoyable books and pictures (and talking about them) can be.

For the reading parent there is now plenty of help. There are lively, sensible, and informed books for parents, such as Leila Berg's *Reading and loving* (1977). Dorothy Butler's *Babies need books* (1980) and *Five to eight* (1986), and Margaret Meek's thorough *Learning to read* (1982). Two colourful and strictly unstuffy periodicals, *Books for your children* (published three times a year) and *Books for keeps* (the magazine of the School Bookshop Association, published six times a year), are designed to help to keep parents up-to-date with new books and current opinions on older ones.

There is no substitute for guidance and sharing ideas at meetings of parents, teachers, librarians, and the like. If nothing else these provide the opportunity to share problems, to reassure, and to make the point that modern children's books are as enjoyable and informative for adults as they are for their intended audience. Such meetings are also an opportunity to exchange ideas and see displays of books and other materials.

As a result of the current concern for shared, paired, partnership reading, a number of groups have arisen to provide assistance and support for parents. Notable examples are Hertfordshire's SHARE (School/Home Achieves Reading Enjoyment), West Glamorgan's CAPER (Children and Parents Enjoying Reading), and Berkshire's PIP (Parents in Partnership). As can be seen by the titles of these groups, emphasis is on shared enjoyment, not a form of 'reading homework'. (See Reading and Language Information Centre, 1987, for details of such groups, and Morgan, 1986 and Bloom, 1987 for advice on parental help in reading—all in 'References and further reading' at the end of this chapter.)

The fortunate pre-school child will have considerable preparation for reading from book activities in the home and at the play-group, and by visiting the public library. Libraries will not only provide a carefully-selected and well-displayed collection of books but also the opportunity to hear stories, paint, draw and make models, make and use puppets, take part in drama sessions, and so on. By the time children go to school they will be used to choosing their own books and will know and enjoy a good range of picture books, stories, and poems. They will be literate.

These kinds of activities are still important once the children are at school. Direct supporting of the learner-reader, by parent, non-specialist teacher, or librarian, can complement what is happening formally in the school. It can consist of telling stories and reading stories—valuable in extending the range of enjoyment and experience of the individual or the group of children. There is a particular need for this if the school programme concentrates on reading-scheme materials that do not offer the narrative, emotional, or language rewards of 'real' books.

The school or public library can cater for confident children by providing a wide range of books and related materials—pictures, videos, music and spoken-word cassettes, computer software, etc.—so arranged and displayed that the young users are not overwhelmed.

There should be story-telling and reading for older children as well as for the young. Activities should extend the awareness of what is available and how it may be used for information and enjoyment. Posters and displays, demonstrations and exhibitions, craft activities, and opportunities for creative writing should all be encouraged.

The basis of such provision should be a welcoming and relaxed environment—an environment offering quietness *and* areas for activity and talk, staffed by people with time to assist groups and individual children. (Automation, computer systems, and so on, should not have been introduced to reduce the number of staff but to free qualified staff to work directly with the library users.) This aspect of the subject is pursued in more detail in Chapter 7 but it is worth stressing the value of the library as neutral territory. If the 'reluctant' learner can be introduced to the library—to see a video or hear some music—he or she may be encouraged by the absence of school pressures and associations of poor performance, and by the interest of an adult who is not, nor does not appear to be, part of the school teaching/discipline system.

Towards reading proficiency

Learning to read is a life-long activity. Schools tend to abandon reading guidance too soon, on the assumption that there is a moment when most pupils can read.

Many young readers are unaware that there are different kinds of reading, appropriate for different tasks: that when seeking specific information one scans and skips; that when reading literature the individual words are important; and that many texts provide a basis or stimulus for the reader's own ideas.

Young readers taught by an approach that stresses decoding (accurate word-for-word reproduction of what is on the page) may fail to become proficient readers. In their excessive respect for the text they may fail to bring their own ideas and their own critical attention to what they are reading. In this way the text is restricting not liberating.

The mature reader, of whatever age, takes liberties with the text: 'Proficient readers can go directly to the meaning of the passage being read, only sampling the print for confirmation of the hypotheses they have made about the meaning intended by the author. In no way is the process conceived of as moving sequentially along the lines of print' (Chapman, 1987, p.6).

The mature reader of literature knows when the author is taking liberties with him or her. The text needs to be watched closely for all may not be as it seems at first. Perhaps the author is being satirical, employing irony, allegory, or ambiguity. Perhaps the author is *not* saying something:

> The reader is in league with the author; this is one of the rules of the reading game, and best learned early. Some children never learn it, not because they cannot read, but because the books they are given do not include this need to attend to what the author is *not* saying—the beginning of an experience that leads to Jane Austen.
>
> (Meek, 1982, p.47)

Each author requires a different relationship with the reader. From Enid Blyton to Henry James, the reader has to appreciate that different things are being expected of him or her. Some writers enter into an intimacy with the reader (Rabelais provides a lively example), some ignore the reader, some (as Laurence Sterne in *Tristram Shandy*) take the reader 'for a ride'.

Such reading requires us to be active and critical. Goodman (1970, p.36) says that 'The reader asks himself not only "Do I understand what this means?" but "Do I buy it?"' Reading is not a passive process. To be passive is, in many instances, to be 'had', to be fooled, or misled. And reading is not an impersonal process. To be successful, reading has to involve the reader. The reader has to make the text something of his or her own, something of him- or herself.

Only as we begin to respond personally to the text's content and open ourselves to its message (irrespective of whether the consequence of this is an acceptance, modification, or rejection of it) do we go beyond a mere decoding or perception of the words and begin to perceive meanings. Then we are bringing our past experiences and present interests to bear on what we read; in short, we are actively involving ourselves in reading, at last able to comprehend what the text means to us, and what it can do to and for us. And this process of commitment to literacy is best and most easily established early in life.

(Bettelheim and Zelan, 1982, pp.36−7)

Once the reader has grasped that there are different kinds of reading (appropriate to different kinds of texts and different purposes), that reading must be undertaken actively and critically, and that he or she has to interact in a personal way with the text, then the reader is becoming proficient.

Perhaps we can now hazard an attempt at defining 'a good reader'. A good reader is one who reads critically, with understanding: 'The interweaving of the reader's meanings and the author's meanings are what we call understanding' (Meek, 1982, p.22)—and with enjoyment. A good reader, now and then, reads material that is just within his or her understanding and, in the process, develops new skills and abilities. Good readers are always in the process of becoming better readers.

A note on readability*

How can the right book be brought to the right reader? The answer is often 'with difficulty'. We would be able to do it more easily if we could not only accurately assess the reading performance of individual children but also the *readability* of particular texts.

Readability, then, is a quality of a book, or any other piece of print, and has been defined as 'the sum total (including interactions) of all those elements within a given piece of printed material that affects the success which a group of readers have with it. The success is the extent to which they understand it, read it with optimum speed and find it interesting' (E. Dale and J. S. Chall, quoted in Gilliland, 1972, pp.12−13). This definition stresses that readability is not merely a matter of *legibility* but also depends upon factors affecting comprehension and motivation.

Such obvious factors as type design and layout clearly affect the legibility of the text. Good type tends not to draw attention to itself, using subtleties of size, serifs, heaviness of stroke, and other characteristics to give ease

*For suggested further reading on readability, see Gilliland (1972), Harrison (1980), and Bentley (1985).

of reading. In a similar way the layout of the type and the distribution of print and space should be such that the reader reads easily but is not made aware of the amount of 'leading' (the white between the lines of type) or the spacing of the words. 'Artistically'-designed editions of books or 'fine editions' are often made difficult to read because the readers, particularly young readers, are made aware of gracefully-designed type, emphasized serifs, and so on, and the use of 'beautiful' space dividers (lines of ornaments) and similar means to produce a book that is fit to frame but not, perhaps, easy to read.

Technical details such as poor paper, irregular or thin inking, and cheap production generally, can affect legibility and in the process the reader's desire and motivation to read the book. A book may look 'too babyish' because of its shape or the type size employed. A book can look 'too dull' because of line length and unrelieved blocks of type. Books can look 'cheap' and unimportant because of misplaced economies over the production, perhaps in the cover design or the quality of the paper.

Other factors that affect readability, but not legibility, are linguistic factors such as size and complexity of vocabulary, complexity and length of sentences, and the complexity of the sequencing and structuring of the paragraphs, the chapters, or the entire book.

Much will depend upon the language ability, the intellectual and life experience of the young reader, and his or her relationship with the writer: 'The readability of the text may be affected by the degree of correspondence between the experience and thoughts recorded in the text and the experiences and thoughts of a reader' (Gilliland, 1972, p.68). These factors have only a limited relationship with the reader's age but will largely determine whether a young reader 'sticks with' or abandons the reading.

The importance of readability has been upheld for so long that all manner of methods have been devised for its measurement. Some have been used informally for many years, subjective assessments such as those made by parents, teachers, and librarians. Some have been constructed on the strictest scientific principles, objective testings, the application of complicated formulae, and tables and charts. The most convincing of the latter have been sentence completion methods like cloze procedure.

In cloze procedure, samples of text selected to be read by a particular reader group (such as nine-year-olds) are tested by representatives of that group. The test pieces have some words removed, perhaps every fifth word, and the tester is required to predict those missing words. The samples are then evaluated in the light of the readers' predictions. If there is low correspondence between the actual missing words and the predictions, then the readability of that text for that particular readership is low. The advantage of cloze procedure is that 'the performance of the reader is being measured on a sample of the text to be read. Few other measures involve the juxtaposition of the intended reader and the text' (Gilliland, 1972, p.105).

Though the scientific matching of book and reader is theoretically possible one can have little faith in it. The complicating factor is the reader's motivation: the effort that children will make if they need to obtain something from a particular book or periodical. Readers will work hard at a text if they need to know something about their favourite football player or team, if they want to know about their favourite singer or group, if they want information for a project that really interests them, or if they need information to make something or improve their performance in some way. A text well within a reader's competence may not invite reading because it is dull, predictable, and appears to have no relevance.

'Can you recommend a book for a five-year-old?' The answer has to be 'no' unless we can be told more about that unique five-year-old. The answer to 'Can you give me a list of the one-hundred best books for seven-year-olds?' has to be 'no, absolutely not'. As Margaret Meek (1982, pp.133−4) says, 'There is, I fear, no short cut for any of us .... We have to know the books and the child to match them in terms of the complicated individuality of both'. That this is so may at first appear disappointing. Once we appreciate that the cause is the complexity—and the unpredictability—of human beings, and the fact that humans are not as 'tidy' as elementary animals or simple mechanisms, then we should be grateful and go about our task with renewed enthusiasm. Those who can't cope would be better employed breeding amoebae.

References and further reading

Bentley, Diana (1985) *How and why of readability*, Centre for Teaching of Reading: University of Reading School of Education. (A brief account of readability.)

Berg, Leila (1977) *Reading and loving*, London: Routledge & Kegan Paul.

Bettelheim, Bruno, and Zelan, Karen (1982) *On learning to read: the child's fascination with meaning*, London: Thames & Hudson.

Bloom, Wendy (1987) *Partnership with parents in reading*, Sevenoaks: Hodder & Stoughton.

Butler, Dorothy (1979) *Cushla and her books*, Sevenoaks: Hodder & Stoughton.

Butler, Dorothy (1980) *Babies need books*, London: The Bodley Head.

Butler, Dorothy (1986) *Five to eight*, London: The Bodley Head.

Chapman, L. John (1987) *Reading: from 5−11 years*, Milton Keynes: Open University Press.

DES (1975) *A language for life*, the Bullock report, London: HMSO.

Gilliland, John (1972) *Readability*, University of London Press.

Goodman, Kenneth S. (1970) 'Behind the eye: what happens in reading', in Kenneth S. Goodman and Olive S. Niles (eds.) *Reading: process and program*, Campaign, Ill.: Commission on the English Curriculum/National Council of Teachers of English, pp.1−38.

Harrison, Colin (1980) *Readability in the classroom*, Cambridge University Press.

Meek, Margaret (1982) *Learning to read*, London: The Bodley Head.

Morgan, Roger (1986) *Helping children read: the paired reading handbook*, London: Methuen.

Open University (1973) *Reading activities with young children*, film no. PE261, Television Programme 4, Milton Keynes.

Reading and Language Information Centre (1987) *Working together: parents, teachers and children*, University of Reading School of Education.

Smith, Frank (1985) *Reading*, Cambridge University Press, 2nd edn.

Waterland, Liz (1985) *Read with me: an apprenticeship approach to reading*, Stroud: The Thimble Press. [A revised second edition of *Read with me* appeared in September 1988, after this book was written.]

Waterland, Liz (1986) '"Read with me" and after' in *Signal*, no.51, pp.147-55.

5

Reading the pictures

The over-used saying (sometimes incorrectly attributed to Confucius) that 'one picture is worth more than ten thousand words' (see Stevenson, 1948, for its actual derivation) is at best a half truth. Its implication that information, experience, and feelings presented in a pictorial form are readily and immediately accessible needs critical examination. However, it doesn't always receive it. As recently as the mid-1980s, Neil Postman (1985, p.79) was writing that 'The six-year-old and the sixty-year-old are equally qualified to experience what television has to offer .... The children see everything it shows'. The brief introduction to Piaget's ideas in Chapter 2, and our realization that as adult readers we cannot read, say, an Ordnance Survey map, a machine drawing, or art forms from cultures not our own with anything like total understanding, should cause us to be cautious and questioning when presented with these assumptions.

The simplest form of reading is often thought to be children 'looking at pictures', but children need to bring a number of skills to the task of reading picture-books if they are to read the pictures with understanding. Children need not only a 'lexicon' of images but also the ability to cope with a number of conventions. For example, the young reader needs to understand the idea of 'sequencing'—the idea that a series of pictures can tell a story, that Quentin Blake's *Mister Magnolia* is not just many separate, entertaining pictures (such as Dick Bruna's *b is for bear*) but that the pictures are telling a story. To read with understanding the young reader has to appreciate that a page of six pictures of a bear may not be about six bears but about one bear and, reading from left to right, that one bear at six different moments in time. Wanda Ga'g in *Millions of cats* presents an opening with ten pictures of kittens, the ones on the left 'thin and straggly' and those on the right 'nice and plump'. The young reader has to be ready to understand that these ten picures are of one kitten thriving on love and care. Carol White was still having problems with sequencing at three-and-a-half-years: 'Again and again, there are ... indications of how slight is the small child's sense of continuity' (White, 1954, p.56).

60

Other conventions that have to be appreciated if meaning is to be obtained from pictures include the following:

- The idea of scaling down, so that a picture of a thing is usually smaller than the thing itself. Indication of perspective presents another convention in which one thing may not in reality be smaller than another but may be shown as such to indicate that it is further away from the viewer.
- The convention of indicating three-dimensional objects in a two-dimensional medium by various forms of shading and hatching.
- The conventions of indicating colour in monochrome illustrations by the use of tones.
- Stylized indications of mental processes and mental states. Strip cartoons of the 'Peanuts' variety employ a vocabulary of such indicators. Here the shapes of the characters' mouths show that they are happy, sad, puzzled or 'miffed', a black cloud over the head indicates that the character is feeling defeated or depressed, the lighted electric-bulb over the head indicates that the character has a bright idea, or the exclamation mark over the head shows that the character is amazed. Notice that these conventions bear limited relation to anything observed in reality: they are conventions, they have to be learnt.
- The idea of 'frozen' action and the devices used to indicate motion. As with the other conventional signs mentioned, the repetition of lines and the distortion of round wheels to indicate that a vehicle is moving bear limited relation to what is perceived in the real world and their meaning has to be learned. Evelyn Goldsmith (1984, p.407) comments that 'Although it appears that some six year olds can understand conventional devices such as speed lines for depicting movement, the most reliable cue is posture, as when people or animals are shown with their limbs in active positions'.
- The convention of showing a part of something and implying the whole. In *The tale of the Flopsy Bunnies*, Beatrix Potter (1909) indicates the presence of Mr McGregor in two illustrations by showing only his boots (pp.27 and 28) and by only his hands in another (p.31). Three-year-old Carol White could not cope with what her mother calls 'decapitated' pictures (White, 1954, p.56).

  Evelyn Goldsmith (1984, p.407), however, found that 'The depiction of objects of which parts are implied as lying beyond the picture frame does not seem to cause any particular problems of interpretation' and comments that a researcher, M. Crago, 'feels that it is a convention

61

which children quickly learn to accept'. The Crago paper referred to here (1979) is a neat piece of research that will reward reading.

The conventions become more complicated as pictures, diagrams, plans, maps, and similar devices in books, films, and videos are required to support the understanding of increasingly-complex things such as structures and processes (from how steel is made and the structure of plant cells, to the relationships between ideas of various kinds and the 'modelling' of mental processes, such as reading).

What do the pictures do?

The first pictures encountered by the youngest readers (and the youngest readers will be *very* young: 'Ideally, a small pile of good books awaits the new baby's arrival' according to Dorothy Butler, 1980, p.27) will be simple, clear pictures of objects to be seen in the reader's immediate world, objects that are becoming familiar in real life. The joy of reading is the joy of recognition at this stage. It is also the joy of reading with and, increasingly, talking with another person. This social aspect of reading, of sharing a pleasurable experience, should begin at this stage. With good fortune it will continue throughout life, in the classroom under the influence of a caring teacher and as an element of mature friendships.

At this stage of recognition, using the *Mothercare* catalogue or the Ahlbergs' witty *The baby's catalogue*, the young reader is learning some of the conventions we have mentioned, is finding a relationship between the content of books and outside reality, building up a useful vocabulary, and—if this is happening in a relaxed and loving environment—having a good time. It is not long before the pictures deal with activities as well as objects: having a bath, going shopping, a visit to the clinic, and walking in the streets and in the country. The good reader is soon able to explore pictures, and to explore and search more detailed and more complicated pictures.

The new picture-reader has a good deal to learn. Evelyn Goldsmith's granddaughter at two-and-a-half years had some difficulty with the convention of 'frozen action', the frozen moment. In a picture in *The house at Pooh Corner* (Milne, 1928) Tigger is falling from a tree (p.69). Katherine said 'He can't get into the tree', and when asked why she replied, 'He's too tired'. For Katherine, Tigger upside down is, presumably, resting. The same problem arose with Quentin Blake's *Mister Magnolia* (1980). In the 'He had green parakeets' opening she could not understand how the bird would get into the cage with his wings spread. The picture was not seen as 'a moment of time' but the wings were assumed to be spread for a long period (Goldsmith, 1984, pp.2–3).

Evelyn Goldsmith (*ibid.* p.387) draws attention to 'the propensity observed in young people to restrict their attention to a small area of a picture'. Like many young children her granddaughter tends to see detail rather than the total picture. Thus, in John Burningham's *ABC* (1964), as the clown is doffing his hat, Katherine at the age of three found 'C' for hat'.

Other problems for Katherine were Burningham's dogs, which she saw as alligators and the notorious iguana became 'I for crocodile'. In the swimming-pool scene in *Mister Magnolia* she thought the puddles were holes.

Pictures then, if they are to be understood and enjoyed, need to be talked about, and talked about most profitably with a more-experienced reader. Exploring pictures and identifying detail in them soon becomes story-telling: 'What is the little girl doing?'; 'Where are the bears going?'; 'Why are the ducklings laughing?'

Pictures and stories

Once books become story books then the pictures have new roles. There are two elements containing the story: the words (heard or read) and the pictures.

In her study of Maurice Sendak, Selma G. Lanes (1981, p.47) speaks of three kinds of story illustration and gives Sendak's evaluation of them: 'From his earliest books on, the artist always rated interpretive [sic] illustrations, pictures that expand a given text and add a new richness of meaning to it, above both narrative illustration which simply mirrors the author's words, and mere graphic decoration'.

Narrative illustration, in the sense given here, is rarely highly thought of by adult critics. It is too reminiscent of the routine, hack-produced illustrations of the past, the kind that were found in school stories and boys' adventure stories, the kind supplied by a succession of artists for the stories of Enid Blyton.

A Henty novel, *At Aboukir and Acre*, provides a typical example: 'Edgar then delivered a blow with all his force', reads the caption and 'William Rainey, R.I.' has pictured a splendid, unarmed, white Edgar using the skill of a trained boxer against a knife-swinging Greek. The Greek looks evil, none too healthy, and (understandably) surprised. The background establishes the location by showing a silhouette landscape of domes and minarets: it could be the back-drop for a village production of the *Desert song*. Thus the illustration contributes nothing to the text, which runs 'Edward [actually Edgar!] lightly sprung aside and avoided the cut aimed at him, and then delivered a blow with all his force just in front of the ear, and the man dropped again as if shot.' (Henty, 1899, facing p.22).

Not only does the picture add nothing to the text but it also doesn't convey as much about the incident as the text. Indeed, it adds next to nothing to the caption.

This is a particularly dated and extreme example of redundancy in illustration. Few modern examples, even those of a routine nature, would be as bad. The most recent illustrations for Enid Blyton's books, those by Betty Maxey, for example, are quite stylish and memorable, even if not outstanding.

Critics probably under-estimate the value of narrative illustration to the young reader, especially the young reader with limited mental picture-making ability. A young reader with limited reading skill may be encouraged in his or her labour by finding the otherwise relentless block of print broken up and relieved with readily-understood pictures. The fact remains, however, that, although Thomas Henry is not an artist of the stature of Sir John Tenniel, Richmal Crompton's William stories seem as incomplete without Henry's illustrations as the Alice books without Tenniel's.

The most successful illustrations, on the other hand, are those that play a full part in the story telling, those that add to the text. Edward Ardizzone (1959, p.41) has said that

In picture books the drawings, of course, are as important as, or more important than, the text. The text has to be short, not more than two thousand words. In fact, the text can only give bones to the story. The pictures, on the other hand, must do more than just illustrate the story. They must elaborate it. Characters have to be created pictorially because there is no space to do so verbally in the text. Besides the settings and the characters, the subtleties of mood and moment have to be suggested.

Ardizzone is not only thinking of picture-books, of course, for his illustrations to *The wind in the willows* and to A. A. Milne's Pooh stories make a similar contribution to the story.

Maurice Sendak also has a clear idea of his role (Lorraine, 1977, p.152): 'To be an illustrator is to be a participant, someone who has something equally important to say as the writer of the book—occasionally something more important, but certainly never the writer's echo'. The illustrations must do something that the text has not done or that the text cannot do: 'You must never illustrate exactly what is written. You must find a space in the text so that pictures can do the work. Then you let the words take over where words do it best' (quoted in Lanes, 1981, p.110).

Sendak, learning from the hard experience of unwillingly providing illustrations for *Nikolenka's childhood*, cites Tolstoy as an example of an author who needs no illustrator: 'Tolstoy, like all great writers, is his own illustrator. When he describes a mother's death and her child's bereavement, heaven knows you don't need a picture. Tolstoy spells it out for the reader in ways that are terribly painful; he leaves no room for pictures' (quoted *ibid*. p.82).

There are then 'tell-tale gaps' (see Chapter 1) in a text for the illustrator as there are for the reader. But they are not the same gaps. There are some books for children that have not been illustrated, and probably should not be illustrated. Examples include Alan Garner's *The Weirdstone of Brisingamen* and Richard Adams' *Watership Down*. Though there is no picture-making task here for the artist, every young reader will make his or her own mental pictures of scenes and of characters' appearances and behaviour.

One would expect author—illustrators to provide some of the best examples of text—picture unity and they do. Beatrix Potter and Tove Jansson are examples, and indeed it would be difficult to think of anyone illustrating the Moomin stories other than their author. More curious examples would be Arthur Ransome's illustrations to his own books. Unique and naïve in style, these 'artless' illustrations remain an important element of the stories and part of the total experience.

What then can the pictures do?

- They can provide the story or the information. In such stories as Shirley Hughes' *Up and up* and Raymond Briggs' *The snowman* the story is told by the pictures, unsupported by text. Information materials can show technical detail and processes, animal behaviour, geographical scenes, and so on, with moving or still pictures and other graphic devices that need the minimum of narrative support.
- They can give the same information as the text, giving the reader two opportunities of gaining clear understanding. This can be useful to the learner-reader, providing extra cues to the text, and to 'the learner-learner'—the person learning to gather and process ideas, or the person entering a new field of knowledge or experience.
- They can extend the information given in the text, as has been seen from the discussion of the picture-book above.
- They can decorate. It would be a mistake to dismiss this, as Selma G. Lanes (1981, p.47) appears to do when she writes of 'mere graphic decoration'. Wanda G'ag, in her *Millions of cats*, uses it to set an appropriately 'folksy' atmosphere. Edward Ardizzone, when he provides miniature sketches for the novels of Trollope, employs decoration to establish or reflect (depending upon how the reader encounters them) the emotional atmosphere of the story. It seems

particularly useful in books of poetry where specific illustrations may intrude and come between the text and the reader's mental imagery, as Brian Wildsmith's do in the *Oxford book of poetry for children*.

- They can, of course, be there to sell the book by making it visually attractive to potential purchasers. This can be helpful to the inexperienced selector *if* the pictures are a true representation of the book.
- They can make the book look attractive to the young reader, and motivate the learner-reader or the resistant-reader to start to read and to continue to read the book. As has been noted before, pictures can break up the text, provide 'landmarks' for the struggling reader, and help in making mental pictures.
- They can help the reader to develop the appreciation and enjoyment of pictorial material by offering a range of rich visual experiences. When reading books illustrated by a Maurice Sendak or a Charles Keeping, children are brought into contact with the visual ideas of artists—ideas of those who would extend their ability to *see* works of art (and the world about them) with increasingly-experienced eyes. Roger Duvoisin (1965, p.25) extends this idea when he speaks of the well-designed page. It not only tells the story 'with more simplicity, more verve, clarity, and impact . . . [it] will also educate the child's taste and his visual sense.'

A book with significant illustrations, like many cinema films, leaves the reader with pictures in his or her mind, a collection of images. The reader develops an ability to respond to the visual as well as the literary.

From the days of Walter Crane, Randolph Caldecott, Beatrix Potter, and Sir John Tenniel, through to Ardizzone and Sendak, children have been presented not with the watered-down and simplified but with the finest graphic work that established artists are able to produce.

Sendak provides a good example. Influenced by a wide range of illustrators and painters, from William Blake to Chagall, his work introduces the young reader to a long tradition of Western art. More specifically, he puts the young reader in touch with the French impressionists in his rich illustrations for Charlotte Zolotow's *Mr Rabbit and the lovely present* (although, strangely, he says that his main influence here was the American naturalistic painter, Winslow Homer), and with the pop art of cinema and food packaging in *In the night kitchen*.

Readability of pictures

Consideration of the readability of pictures immediately raises the issue of the intended audience. Of course, the pictures are for the young readers—or are they? At least three groups need the pictures, and two of those groups are not young readers but are more articulate than them: the artists and those adults who will assess the pictures as critics, potential purchasers, or award panellists.

The artist has needs of self-expression, of visual exploration, and extension. The artist works for personal reasons as well as for recognition, payment, and the children. Even that seemingly most child-aware artist, Dick Bruna, says (1984, p.43), 'I'm sure that if the books hadn't been such a success, I would still be continuing in the same way. It's the only thing I can do'. Artists of the stature of Sendak and Keeping are visual explorers, never satisfied merely to repeat performances, even though those performances are outstanding. The next book must break new ground, provide new insights, provide a new way of looking, or perhaps even a way of re-seeing the familiar. There is a constant danger of losing sight of the young reader, a loss apparent in exquisite pictures that are too complex or more concerned with technique than content; that are too concerned with nostalgia (triggering the adult memory with steam engines and tram-cars, with gas masks and barrage-balloons); books that are aimed at the coffee-table rather than the children; and books that are too 'good' to handle.

This movement away from children is made easier because the adults in publishing houses, criticism, and book-buying, have the critical apparatus and the criteria to assess illustrations as art objects. They are in danger of seeing each illustration as a separate creation, in a picture-frame rather than in a story.

Fortunately there is a kind of illustrator who remains acceptable to the adults and respectful of the young reader. Such illustrators (the Ahlbergs and Shirley Hughes are examples) are true to themselves as creative people, admired by the adult 'establishment', and yet they bear in mind the particular restrictions and opportunities involved when one works for children.

Readability factors

A standard work on the subject, Colin Harrison's *Readability in the classroom* (1980), is typical in giving only scant attention to pictorial material. Illustrations are seen to be a motivating factor for poor readers, but they are otherwise considered to be a distraction and 'do not themselves make the reading level of the prose any lower' (*ibid*. p.127). There is passing reference to the value of illustrations and diagrams in textbooks but otherwise there is no acknowledgement that information can be carried by a range of pictorial forms. The prose does the work, the illustrations interfere at the worst and supplement at the best—so much for pictures in the classroom.

In contrast, a distinguished American book illustrator, Uri Shulevitz, gives considerable attention to readability in his study *Writing with pictures* (1985). He gives high priority to readability, referring to 'the vital aspects of illustration—readability, coherence, and how it relates to the text' (*ibid*. p.11). To Shulevitz, 'A picture's readability depends on the ease and interest with which the viewer can perceive its content and form. The viewer should be able to distinguish easily between static and dynamic elements, between important and unimportant details, between subject and background' (*ibid*. p.121); 'Readability doesn't mean that your picture must look like a poster, full of bold elements that can be perceived all at once. A readable picture can be subtle and delicate, with the viewer slowly discovering details that linger on in the mind' (*ibid*. p.126).

Readability implies that a particular target readership has the experience—the visual, intellectual, and emotional experience—to identify the detail in pictures, to understand what is happening in pictures, and to have some understanding of what is happening 'beyond' the pictures (atmosphere, psychological states, what is being demonstrated in an informative illustration)—in other words, what part the pictures play in the total book, what they contribute.

Basically, the illustrations that are going to succeed with a particular readership by helping the reader to obtain meaning, will use those conventions mentioned earlier in the chapter to indicate, for example, depth (perspective and three-dimensions) and movement, which are within the understanding of that intended audience. Some regard must be taken of the need for a kind of clarity and boldness, a clear differentiation between an object and its background, for example, which need not concern the artist working for adult readers. ('Unclear differentiation between figure and ground makes [a] picture hard to read' (*ibid*. p.173.)

As stated earlier, less attention has been paid to the factors that determine the readability of illustrations than has been given to the readability of text. We assume what the young reader is perceiving. We do not always put our assumptions to the test.

We need to know more about the reader's understanding of still pictures, and more about the understanding of moving and animated pictures. The animated cartoon is rich in conventions, requiring the viewer to understand formalized facial expressions, and action indicators (speed lines, blurs, and so on). The conventions of impermanence, where the cat breaks all its teeth or has all its hair burned off or is squashed flat and, the next moment, becomes whole again, seem to be peculiar to the comic strip and the animated cartoon. At what age can children cope with these conventions?

The film viewer sees a wide range of technical devices—split-screen, slow motion, fast motion, various kinds of fades—that enable the story-teller to indicate that something happened earlier (the 'flash-back') or that something will happen in the future, or that something is being dreamt or fantasized. Sometimes the narrative is intended to puzzle (is he doing it or dreaming it?), sometimes the narrative requires the viewer to know that a sequence is a dream or a memory. The writer's children often ask, when watching television, 'Is this happening *now*?' 'Now' can mean live transmission or 'now' in the story (in other words, not a flash-back). This uncertainty is expressed by both primary and first-year secondary-school children.

How far are viewers at different stages of development equipped for these conventions, one wonders? Do the opportunities provided by computer graphics also present problems to the young viewer unfamiliar, perhaps, with an unusual viewpoint or rapid change of viewpoint?

Readability is concerned with obtaining meaning and also with motivating the intended audience. There has been some attempt to assess children's preferences in terms of subject-matter, illustration style, reproduction processes, use of colour, and so on. The results have been predictable and have not extended our understanding. To learn that children of a particular age group prefer colour to monochrome, strip-cartoon style, and clear and uncluttered illustration is not a revelation.

Another readability factor, and a most important one, is that concerned with cultural factors. Do the conventions previously mentioned have meaning for those from another culture? Are the conventions in materials from other cultures—books from China, animated cartoons from Japan, and so on—understood by young readers in the West, for example? To be specific, do Jewish and Arabic readers have comic strips that read from right to left, as their script does? (The answer, the author is assured, is no, and reminds one of how readily new conventions are learnt by young people).

Pictures for the older reader

It could be argued that since children from about the age of eight years can create their own mental images and since, according to Shirley Hughes (1983, unpaged) 'The best pictures any child sees are in its own head', there is little need for pictures in books for older children.

There is clearly a need for a range of types of graphic devices to support learning, and information and educational materials for older children make full use of such things as photographs of various kinds, maps and charts, graphs, diagrams and technical drawings, flow charts, and other visual means of presenting information, evidence, or data. But is there any need for pictures in support of works of fiction?

To answer in the negative is to say that older children will not benefit from the stunning picture, the arresting image, or the picture that illuminates a story, and that provides a range of visual possibilities. A number of artists have indeed caused some confusion among those who have set expectations by providing picture-books for older readers.

If picture-books are for young children, then what is one to make of, for example, Charles Keeping's edition of Alfred Noyes *The highwayman* or Raymond Briggs' *Fungus the bogeyman*? Charles Keeping's illustrations are clearly not for young children but for older children who are, among other things, coming to terms with the violence and cruelty in our age. It is the imagery of Northern Ireland and of the Middle East made handlable by being associated with a poem and with the past. In a similar way, Raymond Briggs has explored the uncomfortable in picture-books. In that anthology of bad taste, *Fungus the bogeyman*, he brings to the surface a whole range of socially-unacceptable obsessions and images, exposing them within the protective framework of humour. In a similar way, his *When the wind blows* enables the reader to face up to some of the appalling possibilities and realities of nuclear warfare in a way that is just bearable.

Older children, even those with developed visualization abilities, need visual stimulus, need to be presented with new visual ideas, new ways of looking, ways of looking, perhaps, at unfamiliar things—oriental architecture or the workings of a laser application—ways of extending the enjoyment of the seen. Learning to see and remembering to *look* is a life-long process, as the work of any visual artist readily demonstrates. In the spirit of 'why should the devil have all the best tunes?', why should young children have all the best pictures?

References and further reading

Ardizzone, Edward (1959) 'Creation of a picture book', *Top of the news*, Vol.16, no.2, pp.40−6.

Blake, Quentin (1980) *Mister Magnolia*, London: Cape.

Bruna, Dick (1984) in 'Roundhead: Janet Watts talks to the children's author, Dick Bruna', *The Observer*, 13 May.

Burningham, John (1964) *ABC*, London: Cape.

Butler, Dorothy (1980) *Babies need books*, London: The Bodley Head.

Crago, Maureen (1979) 'Incompletely shown objects in children's books: one child's response', *Children's literature in education*, Vol.10, no.3, pp.151−7.

Duvoisin, Roger (1965) 'Children's book illustration: the pleasures and problems', *Top of the news*, Vol.22, no.1, pp.22−33.

Goldsmith, Evelyn (1984) *Research into illustration: an approach and a review*, Cambridge University Press.

Harrison, Colin (1980) *Readability in the classroom*, Cambridge University Press.

Henty, G. A. (1899) *At Aboukir and Acre: a story of Napoleon's invasion of Egypt*, London: Blackie & Son.

Hughes, Shirley (1983) *Word and image*, The Woodfield Lecture VI, Huddersfield: Woodfield & Stanley.

Lanes, Selma G. (1981) *The art of Maurice Sendak*, London: The Bodley Head.

Lorraine, Walter (1977) *'An interview with Maurice Sendak'*, *Wilson library review*, Vol.52, no.2, pp.153−60.

Milne, A. A. (1928) *The house at Pooh Corner*, London: Methuen.

Postman, Neil (1985) *The disappearance of childhood*, London: Comet Books.

Potter, Beatrix (1909) *The tale of the Flopsy Bunnies*, London: Warne.

Sendak, Maurice (1980) in Sheila Egoff, G. T. Stubbs, and L. F. Ashley (eds.), *Only connect: readings on children's literature*, Toronto: Oxford University Press, 2nd edn.

Shulevitz, Uri (1985) *Writing with pictures: how to write and illustrate children's books*. New York: Watson-Guptill Publications.

Stevenson, Burton (1948) *Macmillan's book of proverbs, maxims, and famous phrases*, New York: Macmillan. (This book provides the occidental origin of this familiar quotation. One Fred R. Barnard coined it in a magazine called *Printers' ink*, 10 March 1927, 'and called it "a Chinese proverb, so that people would take it seriously"'.)

White, Dorothy (1954) *Books before five*, London: Oxford University Press/New Zealand Council for Educational Research.

6

'Good' books, 'bad' books

There was a time when a discussion of children's literature or children's reading implied a discussion of 'good' books—and 'good' books implied fiction, indeed, the 'classics' of literature. Librarians and teachers would, with the minimum of encouragement and with formidable confidence, produce lists of 'best' books. Nowadays we are more cautious and questioning in our approach. 'Best' books—best for whom? Best for what?

It *would* be a pity if children did not read, let us say, Beatrix Potter's little books, or *The wind in the willows*, or the Alice books, or Philippa Pearce's *Tom's midnight garden* or Shirley Hughes' *Dogger*. It would be a pity because these books have something special to say about the human condition, about being human beings, and about the power of words and images. These are not merely reading for children but they form part of a shared British culture. These kinds of books have the ability to engage readers (at least some readers) in a particularly intimate and enriching way. They make a permanent and pleasurable addition to ourselves as individuals. We are what we eat, we are told, and we are—at least in part—what we have read.

Having said that, it has to be admitted that there are readers who do not 'connect' with some of the 'best' books. And there are readers who have been deeply moved and impressed in the ways that we have described by books that cannot be described as the best of anything.

The present writer, brought up in a house containing unattractive thrillers of the Sapper era, discovered among that unillustrated and unilluminating Hodder & Stoughton material a correspondence-course crammer, an outline of plane geometry. It was a revelation: that books could contain such mysteries and marvels as diagrams of truncated cones and the like! The book was conceptually too demanding, but it gave a young, reluctant reader new expectations that have lasted a lifetime.

Elaine Moss, in her short article 'The "Peppermint" lesson' (1986) has given us one of the best accounts of the happy marriage of the right reader with the right book. Elaine Moss's daughter, Alison, fell in love with a little picture-book that one might find among the painting-books and the 'join-the-dots' books in a newsagents, but not in a 'proper' bookshop. It was a book that would not reach the reviewers, 'proper' or not. In sentimental, artless pictures and prose, it told the story of a little, unwanted kitten, Peppermint, too thin and unlovely to be sold. The shop owner gives him to a little girl who needs him and cares for him. He is transformed by this loving attention into a fine, prize-winning cat. It was a book without merit, 'hack-written and poorly illustrated . . . artistically worthless' (*ibid*, p.34), yet it had a deep significance and importance for one reader. An unworthy book in many ways, indeed in all perceivable ways, it had engaged one reader in that intimate way that we associate with capital L 'Literature'.

The foregoing discussion leaves one with a number of possibilities. The first is that the 'best' book is the best book for the specific, individual person—the best book that will engage, support, and extend that particular reader. That book may be a well-established, well-regarded book. It may be a book others consider unspecial and undistinguished. The great and life-long affection many have for the books of Enid Blyton cannot be explained in 'pure' literary terms. It should cause us to re-examine our 'pure' literary approach rather than, as in the past, cause us to despair of children's reading tastes.

The second possibility is that there may not be the clear difference between fiction and non-fiction for the young reader that there appears to be for the adult. An 'information' book may provide many of the insights and the language pleasures, and engage the reader in much the same way a literary text does. (Terry Eagleton argues, in his *Literary theory* (1983, pp.1–2) that concern for discrimination between 'fact' and 'fiction', between the 'imaginative' and the 'unimaginative', is of fairly recent origin.)

The 'rewards' of reading

What, therefore, might a 'good' book do for the right reader at the right time? There is a range of possibilities offered in the literature concerned with 'motivation' for reading, some of them more convincing than others.

A 'good' book might provide information of some kind. It might tell the reader about life in the time of Caxton (Cynthia Harnett's *The load of unicorn*) or where babies come from, or how to play chess. More intimately, it may give us greater understanding. If it is written by a true enthusiast, a book will enable the reader to understand why people are committed to the study of the cheetah, DNA, Victorian costume, Alpine plants, or whatever. The history of introducing the animal world to young people is a history of such communication, from the writings of Ernest Thompson Seton, 'Grey Owl', and Cherry Kearton, to the breathless television presentations of David Attenborough and David Bellamy. If it is written by a perceptive and caring author, a story or novel will enable the reader not only to understand but also to empathize with people who are different, or in different circumstances and situations from themselves. The reader *feels* what it is like to be the member of a minority group, to live in wartime, to be handicapped, to be hopelessly in love, or to be bullied at school. Thus the reader of a 'good' book has the opportunity for a quality of understanding shared with the viewer of a particularly sensitive theatre or television play, or a cinema film.

A 'good' book may help the reader to escape from daily cares, pressures, and anxieties. It might provide a temporary suspension of concern about school work, being bullied, or growing up (or feeling one is not growing up). This kind of reading may be the relaxing reading before going to sleep. Such reading is frequently dismissed as 'escapist', the term having pejorative associations with 'cheap', dismissible, trivial, and time-wasting. Perhaps if the term is replaced by 'compensatory' or 'therapeutic' such reading will be considered more sympathetically. The term 'escape literature' is not very useful. Some young readers 'escape' with Enid Blyton, some with *The lord of the rings*: it is the use made by the individual of the material rather than the kind of material that is at issue here. For the young person who finds reading difficult, *Well done, Secret Seven* is not so much escape as very hard work.

A 'good' book needs to have meaning for the individual reader and it must bring meaning to what is experienced in our daily lives. Bettelheim has said in *The uses of enchantment* (1976, p.3) that 'If we hope to live not just from moment to moment, but in true consciousness of our existence, then our greatest need and most difficult achievement is to find meaning in our lives'. It is the argument of this book, as it is the argument of Bettelheim's book, that reading has an important role to play in this process of finding meaning. Other arts play their part (film and theatre, for example) but reading, because it involves the self in such an intimate and exposing way, and because it penetrates to and engages our unconscious, is particularly potent. At worst an escape from life, reading rightly undertaken supports development of the self and the self's need to find meaning.

A 'good' book, no matter how fantastic the scenes or the characters (creatures in space, the inhabitants of Moomin Valley, or talking toys) is essentially concerned with the truth. Writers and illustrators are concerned with finding and telling the truth: the truth as they can see it. The Rustins (1987, p.2) speak of the 'truth-bearing quality' of children's books. Sendak (Lorraine, 1977, p.157) stresses his need to tell the truth:

You must tell the truth about the subject to the child as well as you are able without any mitigating of that truth. You must allow that children are small, courageous people who have to deal every day with a multitude of problems, just as we adults do, and that they are unprepared for most things, and what they most yearn for is a bit of truth somewhere.

A 'good' book is basically and essentially a good story. Whether that story is a folk-tale, an account of how a motor car works, or the childhood of Mozart, it must be structured and it must be entertaining. It is the story that has to be meaningful to, and has to have significance for, the individual reader. A 'good' book must have a story that engages the emotions of the individual reader.

There is a tendency to look upon literature, particularly capital L 'Literature', as something separate from life, but once literature is thought of in terms of story-telling and story-making, then it is seen to be part of a common and seemingly-essential human activity. 'Storying' begins the moment children talk in the playground: 'Let's be . . . '; 'This play on TV was about . . . '; 'Tony took me out last night and . . . '; 'Did you see the match when . . . '. Much of the day is spent story-hearing, story-making, and story-telling. Storying is involved in such private, internal activities as dreaming and fantasizing: 'If I was in charge for a day, I'd . . . '; 'If I had the courage to ask him or her out . . . '. These are not merely story-telling, they are attempts to tidy up external reality, attempts to select, order, shape, often to reshape experiences so that they can be understood, coped with, made more bearable, and ego supporting.

The need to 'story' is demonstrated by the following piece of work by a seven-year-old boy. He doesn't find writing (and he certainly doesn't find spelling) easy, but he has a great *need* to tell his story. This need enables him to persist in his laborious task (the author is indebted to Dafydd Edward Spink for permission to use this story):

the Crocodile and the boy

one day a Boy had a imvertashun to go to a party in Sawth a Merica on the way a crocodil sad Hello Boy do you wont to come Friends yes sad the Boy do you want to come to a Party with my   yes sad the crocodil   comon then ill calle you Croc do you like that name   yes i do What is your name   my name is dafydd you can koll my dafy Comon then   When they came to the partty a nother boy said helo crocodile and the crocodile said my name is croc   okay said the boy croc come and eat   okay Boy   So he did. the end.

(The story is completed by a picture of the crocodile, wearing a party hat, sitting at a table loaded with cakes. By his side a little bird on a stand is singing, and a tiny mouse is searching for fallen bird-food.)

Not only does this represent a great deal of voluntary work, but it also shows how the writer has taken elements from Roald Dahl's *The enormous crocodile*, remodelling the book to meet his own needs. What was a story about an evil-intentioned crocodile that meets a sticky end is now a story about friendship and respect for animals, especially the reptiles that were the writer's current favourite animal. It is worth noting as well that the picture not only confirms that the crocodile enjoyed the party but it also adds a little detail to the wish-fulfilling story: friendship, a party with plenty to eat—and music!

What about 'the classics'?

Before discussing whether they have a place in children's reading today, it is necessary to establish what is meant by 'the classics'. Used loosely and liberally, the term seems to cover any book either written for children or taken by children before about 1900. The 'borrowed' books, like Bunyan's *The pilgrim's progress*, parts of Swift's *Gulliver's travels*, and Defoe's *Robinson Crusoe*, are 'classic classics', since they are already regarded as classics of English literature.

Distinguishing some children's books as 'classics' does serve one valuable purpose: it is the recognition that they are works of merit in their own right. They are not merely stepping stones to 'real' literature, to George Eliot, Henry James, or James Joyce, but they are mature and complete experiences. They stand in the shadow of nothing. To have read *The tale of Peter Rabbit* or the Pooh stories or *The hobbit* is to have had an encounter with fine writing and fine story-telling. *Middlemarch* and *The golden bowl* are not the same but, though they are a good deal longer, they are not different in kind or quality.

For the 'purist', applying a strict and arbitrary cut-off date such as 1900 creates the need of another category that will enable the capturing of examples already cited. With implications sometimes of the second class, these later books are categorized as 'the modern classics', a categorization that also enables the critics to play their game of 'spot the classic'. Among the 'modern classics' so far spotted would be *The wind in the willows*, the Pooh stories, *The hobbit*, the Narnia books, *Charlotte's web*, and *Tom's midnight garden*. This is an amusing adults' game with limited value.

Sometimes one feels, and many children must feel, that the label 'classic' is applied to any book that is dull (in appearance at the very least), austerely impressive, dauntingly rich in long sentences and difficult words, and slow in terms of incident and action. It is a label applied to any book adults read in some distant childhood, adults who are out of touch with the current wealth of books (to say nothing of other media) that are available to young children today.

The corollary to this is that few books that are too enjoyable, too funny, or too popular could possibly be 'classics'. The books of Roald Dahl are in the group of books that, due to their appeal to young readers, and perhaps their iconoclastic treatment of the adult world, are suspect as far as critics and prize panels are concerned. Something so enjoyed could not be sound.

There is a certain medicinal thinking behind the labelling, a feeling that a book that is difficult to read and difficult to obtain meaning and enjoyment from, must be good for young people in some way. Perhaps it sharpens and develops reading, decoding, and comprehension skills. Perhaps, one is tempted to retort, much in the spirit of Mary Jane and 'lovely rice pudding again', it helps to build up a life-long resistance to anything judged to be 'a classic'.

'Classic' is an adult classification having some value for adults as critics, evaluators, or selectors. The 'classics' do provide certain standards of excellence. Beatrix Potter's little books provide a model of the economic use of precise language; E. Nesbit sets standards of pace, intimacy with the reader, vivid immediacy, and dialogue; Frances Hodgson Burnett shows how it is possible to hold and express beliefs (such as the power of Nature) and still remain in control; Robert Louis Stevenson demonstrates the spirit-stirring power of adventure, a sort of basic human need to succeed and to survive gloriously; Arthur Ransome illustrates how a matter-of-fact tone can match the no-nonsense approach of children; and so on. This is a different thing from recommending the works of those writers to children in today's world. Excellence for adults? Excellence despite the absence of young readers?

One of the problems in the recognition of 'classics' is that the awe-inspiring label discourages periodical re-assessment. Thus, once appointed 'classics', such books as *The children of the New Forest*, *The water babies*, *Lorna Doone*, *At the back of the north wind*, and *Little women* retain the title. Who dares to question, let alone contradict, the verdict of time and a succession of prestigious critics? Certainly children are unlikely to challenge adult opinion, being more likely to decide that they are poor readers rather than that a 'classic' is a poor book. The exception is the competent and confident young reader like Sharon in Donald Fry's study (1985, p.115), who sums up *The children of the New Forest* with the words 'a lot to read for a little bit to happen'.

The problem with approaching children's reading from a 'classics' approach—identify the best, the books 'of transparently permanent greatness' (Rosenheim, 1980, p.51) and give them to the children—is that it places emphasis on the book, on the literary work, and not on the needs and tastes of the individual reader. It places emphasis on external evaluation and it undervalues the individual young reader's assessment.

If we must have 'classics' let us accept James Steel Smith's definition of a book that 'provides some special imaginative experience which the child is not likely to get from other sources—or at least in the same degree of intensity—and which it would be a shame for him to miss' (1967, p.121). And having accepted it, let us admit that the book that gives this experience to the individual young reader who needs it or will benefit from it, may not be what we (outside the experience) might recognize as a 'classic'.

Reading 'rubbish'

Childhood is short. Although it is an intense period of development and although it provides the basis of values, attitudes, and feelings—as well as darker things like repressions and obsessions—that may last a lifetime, it soon passes.

Adults, particularly caring parents, appreciating its transience and its value, have the feeling that every moment of childhood should be spent in activity that is clearly worthwhile and rewarding in some way. There is no time for 'rubbish'; there is no time for reading 'rubbish'.

'Rubbish' has been defined by Peter Dickinson (1973, p.101) as 'all forms of reading matter which contain to the adult eye no visible value, either aesthetic or educational'. A similar definition is given by Aidan Chambers (1983, p.102): 'By "rubbish" adults usually mean literature which in their judgement lacks any artistic, moral or educational value'. It is a label that can be quickly and uncritically applied to a range of reading: such things as comics and fan magazines, the Christmas annuals, TV and cinema spin-offs, albums of stickers, the works of Enid Blyton, and so on. Time saved should be spent reading material of tested value, of literary value—the 'classics', the well reviewed, the prize winners.

There is something of a double-values system at work here. Adults tend to dismiss as worthless much that their children read, while having a nostalgic affection for similar material read in their own childhood. It is a case of children should not waste their time reading *The Dandy*, nor must they interrupt us adults as we reminisce about Desperate Dan and Korky the Cat.

'Rubbish' is an adult verdict sometimes based on the assumption that what is unrewarding for the adult reader must be unrewarding for the young reader. It is applied by adults who read a wide variety of material with a wide variety of 'value' (the newspaper headlines, a new best-selling novel, the horoscope for the day, financial annual reports, personality gossip, a Jane Austen novel, holiday brochures to exotic places, hints on cooking rice) but feel that children should only read things of lasting value and of clearly-identified worth. It is as if the organized adult only listens to the late Beethoven quartets and has no associations with popular songs or dance music, light opera or musicals, hymns Ancient or Modern.

As we have already established, the 'good' reader is the omnivorous reader, prepared to tackle anything in sight. How else is the good reader to establish what is good for him or her individually? How else is the good reader to learn the difference between what others—critics for example—say is good, and what is personally judged to be good? How else is the individual to discover individual tastes and preferences? Aidan Chambers (1983, p.103) notes that 'Wide, voracious, *indiscriminate* reading is the base soil from which discrimination and taste eventually grow'. (The adult readers might like to list those books, and other reading matter, for which they have a particular affection or which they feel have made a contribution to their lives, and then check to see how many of them would be considered to be of the highest literary worth.)

The controversy about worthwhile reading often revolves around the books and stories of Enid Blyton, so these will be given some attention. Her writings clearly and demonstrably have limited literary worth. As a collection of writings they are repetitive, unadventurous, and undemanding. Individually they are slow; the characters are wafer thin and have little individuality; there is no evidence that the author is excited by language; there is little evidence that she has a developed sense of humour. So much for the adult assessment of the total output of Enid Blyton.

The young reader, tackling his or her first Famous Five or Secret Seven book, encounters a story of breathtaking originality and excitement. A group of children and a dog go to a lonely old house on the sea coast for their summer holidays. Their parents are called away and they are left in the care of servants. It is raining. They are bored and start to explore the house. One of them activates a secret latch, book shelves swing aside to reveal a flight of descending stone steps. With torches (all story-book children carry torches—torches with sound batteries, too) they explore the dark tunnels . . . .

If this were a story by a 'serious' writer the critics would pursue the symbolism of hidden latches and dark tunnels as diligently as the children pursue the gang of international smugglers discovered in the cave at the end of the tunnel. This, however, is a story by Enid Blyton so it couldn't contain any symbolism, could it?

The young reader wonders how one human being could invent such an interesting story, and write it all in words that are so easily read. There have been so few reading problems in the whole hundred-and-odd pages that the story has been free to come to life, you can see it all, enjoy it all: 'Dear Miss Blyton, I think your stories are really exciting!'

Effortlessly read and soon completed, the stories are indeed 'sunny', presenting a secure world of little anxiety, limited emotion, and no real trauma. No writing specifically designed to calm and assure could improve on these positive, jolly tales. 'But life is not like that. People—young people—are not like that', the critics start to cry, forgetting that many children are painfully (the word is carefully chosen) aware of the fact. They know about the world. They need to visit the temporary dream world of confident and cared-for children—and the dog.

The Rustins have written (1987, p.61) that Enid Blyton was 'apparently uninterested in emotional pain'. It may be that her devoted young readers need respite from emotional pain.

Aidan Chambers (1983, p.105) finds a different reason for the popularity of the Blyton books, a reason related to the theory of 'tell-tale gaps'. He says

> I suspect that [the] very absence of quality is what makes such stuff attractive to children, not just because it is easy to read, undemanding, untaxing, but because the simplistic plots and characters leave children free to embroider and enrich the stories *in their own way* as they read. The author provides an outline; the young reader uses the outline on which to graft his own refinements.

Donald Fry (1985, p.83) raises another value in reading rubbish. One of the young readers in his study, Joanne, is reading James Herbert's horror book, *The rats*, and he comments that '*The rats* is trash; but from the practice of reading trash a reader can still derive experience of fiction applicable in later reading. It is often in popular fiction that we see most plainly the conventions that writers handle and readers learn, and where literary competence begins to be developed'. It is interesting to note that while Joanne is reading *The rats*, circulating in the classroom as a sort of illicit 'dare' read, she is also reading the books of one of her favourite writers, Beatrix Potter.

Children read a wide variety of things, from the back of the cereal packet to *The Dandy*, from a page of the daily newspaper to something written by Roald Dahl, and who is to know what will trigger off ideas, possibilities, expectations, or activity? Rubbish has a place in this process of stimulation.

'Bad' books

Despite what is written above, there are bad book elements in Enid Blyton's stories—if we define bad books as those that limit readers' expectations of themselves and of others.

Bad books include those that limit girls' ideas of their independence and self-determination. Enid Blyton offers us the independent girl as something of a freak: 'George', the independent girl as 'problem', even if she is more interesting and more individual than the other characters. One has to search the memory to find the names of the rest of the Famous Five.

The issue of sexual stereotyping is not confined to writing of Enid Blyton's quality. In their examination of the Narnia stories, the Rustins (1987, pp.47−8) found that C. S. Lewis gave distinct roles to the male and female characters: 'The sexual division of labour is entirely conventional as is the apportionment of sensitivity and intuition to girls and courage and decisiveness to the boys'. 'Lewis attributes [the] capacity for suffering to the girls, and an active fighting role to the boys' (ibid. p.53).

Notice that this stereotyping works against both sexes. The sensitive, the unsure, the non-aggressive boy reader must often feel inadequate when faced with the 'ideal boy' of stories. There is a need for books like Gene Kemp's *The turbulent term of Tyke Tiler* and the Pippi Longstocking stories of Astrid Lindgren, which question the imposed sex-roles of girls. There is also the need for books like Ivan Southall's *Josh*, which recognizes the existence of sensitive and non-fighting boys.

Bad books are those that limit readers' expectations of themselves, and those that limit expectations of others, especially those of another ethnic background, religion, sex, or social class. The family with a different ethnic background next door can be viewed positively—potentially offering opportunities for new ideas and new experiences—or negatively in terms of 'problems' of difference. The attitudes of authors of stories the young read or hear, whether prejudiced or condescending or exaggeratedly 'socially aware', are readily perceived and are influential, even when they are half hidden.

Apart from the bad, there is another category that might be called the gloriously bad or the awfully bad: one thinks of all those collections of groan-producing puns and nonsensical jokes and riddles. What is white on top and white on the bottom, green in the middle, and leaps about the room? A frog sandwich, of course. Janet and Allan Ahlberg have raised the genre to new depths with *The ha ha bonk book* and *The old joke book*. Perhaps the comics are in this category too, not merely 'rubbish' but collections of rampantly-bad jokes and celebrations of poor taste.

There is also the mediocre. The mediocre does not offend, it is not controversial, and it certainly does not challenge. It is respectable, comfortable, and bland:

> What I principally object to are all our dreary, smug books about growing up and coming to terms with oneself, that ... are merely another brand of conformity .... It's the mediocre that drags us all down to a common denominator; ... that deprives us of judgement; ... that particularly deprives us of a sense of humour.
>
> (Egoff, 1972, p.3439)

The mediocre is less acceptable than the down-right bad because it sometimes masquerades as something worth while. As it does not offend it tends to survive and to remain to waste readers' time. While the readers are reading a weak, Tolkien-influenced story, or a weak abridgement of a book, they could be tackling the original.

So much for the various qualities of books. Sheila Egoff (1972, p.3436) provides the categorizing test when she says 'A fine book sends me rushing to share it, with anyone I can find, child or adult; a mediocre book sets my teeth on edge, and a poor one makes me laugh'.

In offering children a range of materials, with a range of quality, the teacher, librarian, or parent is helping to bring about discerning, entertained, and informed young readers: young people equipped and encouraged to evaluate and to question. The act of faith required to permit children to judge and to choose is a simple one. Most children are able to judge the true and the false, what is relevant to their needs, what reflects a reality they know, what is merely fashionable, what is weak, and what is too idealistic.

Children are not as innocent or as vulnerable as some would suppose, or wish to suppose. They can be damaged by those who are over-protective as well as those who neglect or abuse them. Over-protection from prejudice or cruelty, for example, can lead to their being offered a picture of a world they realize is divorced from the real world around them, from the harsh realities of the world news, and from the harsh realities of people's treatment of people. Books and other materials that are a world away from truth are inhibiting, if not damaging. Most children do not need them.

References and further reading

Bettelheim, Bruno (1976) *The uses of enchantment: the meaning and importance of fairy tales*, London: Thames & Hudson.

Chambers, Aidan (1983) *Introducing books to children*, London: Heinemann Educational Books, 2nd edn.

Dickinson, Peter (1973) 'A defense of rubbish', in Virginia Haviland (ed.) *Children and literature: views and reviews*, Glenview, Ill.: Scott, Foresman, pp.101—3.

Eagleton, Terry (1983) *Literary theory: an introduction*, Oxford: Basil Blackwell.

Egoff, Sheila (1972) 'If that don't do no good, that won't do no harm: the uses and dangers of mediocrity in children's reading', *Library journal*, Vol.97, no.18, pp.3435—9.

Fry, Donald (1985) *Children talk about books: seeing themselves as readers*, Milton Keynes: Open University Press.

Lorraine, Walter (1977) 'An interview with Maurice Sendak', *Wilson library review*, Vol.52, no.2, pp.153—60.

Moss, Elaine (1986) 'The "Peppermint" lesson', in her *Part of the pattern: a personal journey through the world of children's books, 1960—1985*, London: The Bodley Head, pp.33-4.

Rosenheim, Edward W. (1980) in Sheila Egoff, G. T. Stubbs, and L. F. Ashley (eds.), *Only connect: readings on children's literature*, Toronto: Oxford University Press, 2nd edn.

Rustin, Margaret and Rustin, Michael (1987) *Narratives of love and loss: studies in modern children's fiction*, London: Verso.

Smith, James Steel (1967) *A critical approach to children's literature*, New York: McGraw-Hill. (Chapter 6, 'Children's classics', is an astute and witty review of this topic.)

7

Children as customers

What follows may suggest that we have moved a long way from the consideration of reading. This is not really the case. If we are to support children in their reading we need to encourage them into libraries, to assure them that libraries are pleasant places, and that librarians are pleasant people equipped by education, training, attitudes, and commitment to serve them.

If we are to encourage reading for information, education, and enjoyment, then libraries themselves—the stock, the staff, and accommodation—need to be informative, educative, and enjoyable. Bettelheim and Zelan (1982, p.305) speak of stories that treat children 'with dignity and [accord them] the respect they deserve'. Libraries should do that too.

This chapter is written with humility and with admiration by a former librarian whose strategy, when dealing with troublesome readers, was to go to pieces and leave it to Nancy. Nancy was a rather frail-looking, young, 'unqualified' assistant who had all the skills of defusing potentially-nasty situations. She generated calm and common sense and managed to overwhelm conflict with goodwill. She appeared to be born with these gifts. She should have been crowned 'Queen of Merseyside'.

Those of us who did not have Nancy's gifts found little to help in our training or in our reading. A pamphlet published by the American Library Association, *Patrons are people: how to be a model librarian*, originally published in 1945 and revised in 1956, illustrates the approach of the time: 'Whether six or sixty, a person is a person and should be treated as such, so the Model Librarian avers. In dealing with children she follows the same general rules as she would use in dealing with their parents . . . . She treats them with courtesy and consideration . . . . She respects a child's privacy' (p.27). Much of this is sound but the atmosphere is that of a genteel and idealistic world, a world less harsh than our own.

It is significant that when a British version of this booklet appeared in 1953, *The reader and the bookish manner* (Association of Assistant Librarians), it contained no mention of children. This is, perhaps, a reflection of the status of children's libraries and children's librarians just after the war. There is little in print to this day, however, that discusses desirable approaches to the young library user—and the troublesome young library user.

The UK Library Association *Code of professional conduct* (1983) does not make separate mention of young people but provides the important principle that 'Members' primary duty when acting in the capacity of librarian is to their clients' (para.2d). This statement is not expanded to discuss the conflicting duties that face those who serve children—duties to the parents, duties to the school, and so on—but it is a good beginning. It uses the term *client* and the term *client* suggests a particular kind of relationship. It implies a certain *commitment* to the user and his or her needs, and it implies a particular kind of responsibility to ensure that the user has the skills to obtain what is needed: that is, to obtain the right information or material, in the right form, so that the user can benefit from it.

As the earlier quotation from *Patrons are people* implies, a young person enters the library as an individual, independent person with the right to a full, professional level of service. The fact that some young people leave much to be desired in terms of appearance, behaviour, and attitudes (perhaps personal hygiene, too) is as irrelevant in this context of quality of service as the fact that many adult users of services are odd, rude, and aggressive. There is always the possibility that young people will grow out of *their* peculiarities.

While in the library, the young user is an *individual*—not a member of Miss Jones's class, or one of the Polish community, or 'a typical teenager', or so-and-so's daughter or son. He or she does not bring associations of failure or disadvantage, of prestige or advantage into the library. The library is neutral ground and should be welcoming, catering for the poor reader, the poor learner, the gifted, the disturbed, and the insecure.

We are already falling into the trap of describing an ideal world and suggesting that it exists. Unless we have attitude training in preparation for our work, we are quite likely to bring with us into the library our prejudices and biases.

Expectations can be damaging, especially when they are based on prejudice. Not all young people are unruly, rude, and uninformed. Many *are* noisy, dirty, and uninformed, as are many adults, but they may be bright and attractive people at the same time. A number will be vicious. A larger number will be socially assured, responsible, and remarkably knowledgeable.

The problem customer

Whereas we can rarely help the 'delinquent' adult, we have some responsibility to young people with particular problems or insecurities that show in 'anti-social' behaviour and attitudes. They at least deserve our patience and understanding.

One principle is to suspend judgement. Appearances of being vicious, mindless, or mediocre can be deceptive, and the deception is often studied and rehearsed. Teenagers seem particularly unwilling to be seen as the caring and bright people they often are. Even the would-be socially superior, the boastful, and the priggish may be found to be quite agreeable people once they have relaxed. Of course, there are those young people whom only a parent could love. They, too, have a right to the best service we can offer. If it is hard work, give yourself a cup of tea and a medal after the encounter.

What about the destructive and the vicious? Libraries are no longer places of quiet:

> In line with the recent emphasis on leisure in our society, libraries have made a concerted effort to attract young people. We have provided comics, magazines, records and cassettes; we have installed comfortable seating and modern furniture, and have laid on numerous events and activities: we have been successful in updating our image, but one of the consequences of our success has been the degree to which we have attracted the rowdier elements of the local youth.
>
> (Nottinghamshire County Library Service, 1983, para.2.3)*

When dealing with the violent and destructive there seem to be a number of rules to be followed:

- Act early rather than late.
- Try reason. If it fails, be decisive, and be decisive quickly.
- Be sure that when you do something irreversible, such as destroying any possibility of a relationship by calling the police, you realize what you are doing.
- By sure that you can live with the results of your actions. Try to avoid creating a group of youngsters that is hostile to the library: they are known as 'vandals'.

---

*An excellent report, as are those of other library services (e.g. Hertfordshire) that have considered the problem. Much of the material in this section comes from MacLeod (1986) and 'How to combat vandalism?' (1986).

- Seek all the allies you can find: users, social workers, youth workers, school psychologists, probation staff, and teachers. Ask for advice and guidance but try to ensure that the policy decision-making and the responsibilities remain in your own hands.
- Leave Nancy to do it. That is, let the person who is qualified by personal qualities, by experience or by circumstances (for example, someone who is part of the local culture) handle the situation, even if they don't have the appropriate ranking in the staff hierarchy. Having demonstrated their ability to cope with difficult users, ensure that such people's worth is made known—and is rewarded.

British librarians seem to have been slow to react to the increase in the numbers of problem customers. Few libraries have guidelines or provide training programmes. The Library Association of the UK has only fairly recently (June 1987) produced an 'advice note' concerning aggressive and unacceptable behaviour in libraries.

Librarians in the USA faced up to the problems rather earlier, and there is some literature offering guidance from the late 1970s. Much of it seems realistic and sensible: 'Do not threaten to call the police. If you feel the need to, just call them' (Elliott, 1982, p.8); 'Adolescents need to be treated with respect and are very sensitive to being patronized. They like to test authority figures—the librarian. Don't take their behaviour personally' (*ibid*. p.9).

This advice seems to be based on experience and the real understanding shown when such phrases as 'the usual juvenile restlessness' are used. It may be distinguished from this kind of guidance from another American source: 'Separate any group of offending youths, dealing with them on a one-to-one ... basis' (Grotophorst, 1979, pp.349−50). Good advice based on sound theory, perhaps, but the writer does not go on to say how this separating might be accomplished!

The summary of this American experience seems to be as follows:

- Anticipate problems. This is not an area where policies and procedures can be formulated *after* a few incidents have been experienced. The first incident may be one endangering life or property.
- Define what is acceptable and what is intolerable behaviour in such areas as violent language, noise level, drug-and-drink-influenced behaviour, and sexual harassment. There is a useful guiding principle behind the phrase 'inappropriate use of the library'.
- Define the role of the librarian. There is some role conflict when the librarian educated in a tradition of user-helping and support finds a situation calling for regulation (even law enforcement) that may appear to be a negative role.

- Know your law, local bye-laws, and national legislation. Under what circumstances is the member of the public breaking the law? Under what circumstances is the member of staff breaking the law? 'Barrack-room lawyers' are to be found among the youngest members of the population. In summary, don't find yourself being accused of assaulting a young person. The most vicious can suddenly look very prim when assuming the role of the victim.
- Have an agreed, known policy. A corollary of this (especially for staff in non-violent areas of the community—or the library itself) is: ensure that the staff take the policy seriously. There is a danger of an 'oh-it-will-never-happen-here' kind of attitude.
- Train all the staff. Do not overlook porters, caretaking staff, security officers, and so on. Sessions should include attitude training, assertiveness training, and preparation for the counselling of victims of violent and abusive behaviour, both users of library services and staff members.

A source already mentioned provides this summary for those who have to deal with the immediate problems (Elliott, 1982, p.10):

1 Be calm and impersonal.
2 Set limits and stick to them.
3 Repeat your request (to leave, etc.) if necessary.
4 Do not argue with outrageous statements.
5 Be explicit—mention the problem behavior.
6 Offer a choice of action—change or leave.
7 Avoid humor or personal remarks.
8 Alert another staff member if you notice someone acting strangely.
9 Be considerate.

The final note here is an appropriate one. To be firm and remain courteous is the great art, especially when you feel threatened or are greatly provoked. Part of the art is to avoid creating a permanent conflict with a section of the community. The writer once witnessed the eviction of a young reader from a London branch library. The child was clearly known to be a trouble-maker and, as he was about to enter the library, he was 'told to leave'—a quite inadequate description of the drill-sergeant bellow produced by the woman librarian on counter duty. The message had the quality of directness and unambiguity, but a gauntlet had been thrown down that no self-respecting, authority-bating child could ignore.

If all else fails, try to adopt the attitude of Betty Vogel (1976, p.66) who says: 'Instead of being irritated by [difficult] patrons, we should exult in their outrageous humanity—in the rich diversity of human personality

that we are daily privileged to observe'. This may prove difficult if they
have you pinned to the wall.

'The successful children's librarian'

It is obvious that the success of a library service depends on both the quality
of the materials that make up the stock and the quality of the staff who
administer and promote the service.

What character, what gifts should the staff possess? Library literature
is rich in descriptions of 'the ideal children's librarian'—Janet Hill in her
seminal *Children are people* (1973, Ch.1) has discussed a number of them.

The basic assumptions are that the librarian will be a woman
(woman=child carer) and a very special kind of person. In 1903 John
Ballinger spoke of 'a sympathetic, well-educated woman, with organizing
ability and a good temper' (p.554) and W. C. Berwick Sayers in 1932
described 'A person of good education, solid nerves, and attractive to
youngsters' (p.166). In 1961 Lionel McColvin wrote that 'the successful
children's librarian' must have 'common sense, which means that she must
be able to take things as they are, to do simply what the situation requires,
without fuss, to give and take, to be tolerant, to be practical. Then she
must be placid and patient' (p.97). Leonard Montague Harrod, in his
remarkably anachronistic *Library work with children* (1969, p.24), saw
the good children's librarian as

> primarily and fundamentally one who is friendly, a good mixer, of
> sound character and having much commonsense; she must be patient,
> not easily put out by misbehaviour or pressure of work, remaining calm
> at all times; she must like children and be tolerant of them and their
> ways and also of her colleagues; she must be willing to turn her hand
> to any job that needs to be done in the department even if it is normally
> done by people junior to herself.

(As an aside, one wonders if Mr Harrod would have written in similar
terms about the work of the reference librarian or any other senior post
usually occupied in that period by a man.)

The librarian serving children was, then, to be a most unusual person,
a paragon, a sort of *bibliothécaire* Florence Nightingale, but without her
disturbing leadership and reformist qualities. One wonders what young
library users would make of such an unnaturally placid, unearthly
character.

Observation suggests that young people are most at ease and most open
with adults who treat them 'casually' and as equals, who do not indulge
them, act in a condescending way, or look upon them as something
'special'. Many busy working people have this quality of appeal,

workpeople who will share an interest in what they are doing in an office or down a hole in the street. Many settled childless people, the Edward Lears and Richmal Cromptons of our time, have this appeal. Sadly, many who think they are 'children people' are not (to borrow Berwick Sayers' phrase) 'attractive to youngsters'.

Rather than all the rare qualities discussed, the person serving young people in the latter part of the century needs to be able to work in a no-nonsense way with young people, to be a good manager prepared to fight for a fair share of the funds, to ensure that staff are able to devote a generous amount of time to users of the services in groups and as individuals, and to ensure that there is a good stock of books and other materials to explore. In brief, to ensure that the services are at least as efficient and effective as those provided for adult users—those who are, in short, politically more powerful.

In order to do this it is also necessary to keep aware of the context, or environment, in which reading and library use take place. It is essential to keep in touch with the latest books and reading tastes, but it is also important to be aware of the cultures of the home and the community, of young people's television viewing and cinema habits and tastes, the range of musical interests, dress preferences, current hobbies, sports, and pastimes, and the toys and play activities in fashion. It would seem difficult to provide a relevant stock of materials and range of services without being aware of these changing factors.

It is also essential for those providing services to young people to cling onto their adulthood. When dealing with younger age groups there is a particular danger of assuming a certain tone of voice and a certain kind of authority. There is less danger of this today when television presenters, for example, offer the image of the generous brother and sister rather than the understanding uncle or aunt. The danger is still there, however, especially if colleagues in adult services are under the impression that all who work with children are slightly fragile—and 'potty' with it.

One solution to the problem of stereotyping, and of endangered adulthood, is to rotate staff so that all have the opportunity to serve young people for short periods in their own particular way. One revelation is when the member of staff who seemed most unsuitable, perhaps cynical and short tempered when dealing with adults, is found to have the ability to engage with young minds. However, this does not always happen.

Attitudes and approaches
Margaret Donaldson has stated (1978, p.111) that there is 'a fundamental human urge to make sense of the world and bring it under deliberate control'; 'a fundamental human urge to be effective, competent and

independent, to understand the world and to act with skill' (*ibid*, p.113). This urge is not something that appears when we are at school or later—it operates from birth, if not before.

Those who meet the needs of this urge are, on the whole, balanced, satisfied, and fulfilled, growing and developing throughout life. Those who lose or cannot meet the urge become 'defeated', become dependent, destructive, or, if not apathetic, at least dismissive.

As parents, teachers, and librarians, we wish to encourage young people and to support them in their search for understanding, expression, and confidence. For librarians, giving support means not only the application of our expert knowledge and experience to provide materials and services but also, and more particularly, providing caring interest, belief in the individual's importance, and confidence in the individual's abilities. It is the provision of time, attention, positive attitudes, and security.

Giving support means taking an active and genuine interest in whatever concerns the young reader. (This is not difficult since young people's enthusiasms are persuasive and infectious.) Such interest gives the activity and the young person status—and, of course, gives all parties the opportunity to learn and to understand.

There can be no condescension, fuss, or invasion of privacy; the support must be based on respect for the individual, recognizing the significance in what individuals do and say. In their work with children, Bettelheim and Zelan would approach a problem by asking ' "What is the child feeling and what is its importance?" And we should then find an answer that is valid from *his* point of view, rather than an answer that simply reflects *our* point of view' (1982, p.35). (The authors' respect for children is further demonstrated by the attention they give to misreadings—'miscues'—and blocking. When a learner-reader miscues he or she is 'projecting important personal meaning into the story'—*ibid*. p.152.)

In a similar way we sometimes need to remind ourselves that young readers have ideas that are worth consideration, and that the administratively-convenient solution to a problem may not be the most valuable one. Respect for young readers is often expressed by working with them as distinct from working for them; asking them rather than telling them. Immaturity does not mean that they have no worthwhile ideas. By our attitudes we sometimes suggest that they have no ideas at all.

Acknowledging, then, the importance of positive attitudes in those who work with young readers, how can we ensure that all staff possess such attitudes? We can, of course, select staff who are 'young-user-friendly', and then try to ensure that they remain so by encouragement. We can also provide training opportunities.

An attitude-training programme for those serving young readers would be expected to cover the following:

- User-friendliness and what this specifically means in the context of services to young people.
- User-awareness—familiarity with young people's tastes in such things as TV viewing, music, clothes and make-up, and leisure activities, as well as reading tastes and habits.
- The exposure of prejudice and of acting upon stereotypes (especially those promoted by 'the media'). Staff need to be made aware of the indicators that trigger off their own prejudices—snotty noses, nose- and ear-rings, coloured hair, leather jackets, elaborate and expensive school uniforms, gum-chewing—all those things that set off an expectation of a certain kind of behaviour, regardless of the individual young person's personality.
- Communication skills: establishing relationships and giving guidance and information. Awareness that young people seem to be particularly able readers of 'body language' and other non-verbal revelations of attitude.
- Relationship matters, formerly considered in only a limited way as 'discipline'. Discussing the relationships of the librarian with the users is one way of discussing the role of the librarian, a way that keeps the reader in the forefront of the issue.

Special children, special readers*

There has been limited mention of special children (or children with special needs) so far in this book. All children, it might be said, are special; with good fortune, they are special to those who parent them, to those who help them to learn, to those to whom they are clients, and to themselves. Some are special because of the needs that arise from some physical or mental handicap; some are special because of a particular gift; some because no one treats them as though they are special.

It is the aim of the librarian, as of others, to limit handicap. It is not entirely true that people are as handicapped as we, the comparatively unhandicapped, are prepared to handicap them, but there is more than a grain of truth in that statement.

---

*This section owes a great deal to the work of Margaret R. Marshall, especially her *Libraries and the handicapped child* (1981). I am also pleased to acknowledge the help of Helen Steele who taught me so much about handicap and achievement in one short meeting.

'Access' has been a key-word in the discussion of the handicapped in libraries, not only access to the building but also access to the materials and services and to the information, knowledge, and entertainment contained within those materials. Access is also discussed in relation to those who cannot get to the library—the housebound and the institution-bound, those who have limited mobility, and those whose behaviour is 'unorthodox' in some way.

Attitude training is necessary for all who are going to encounter young people as customers, and all who are going to encounter special children. In both cases this means training for most of the staff, from porters and maintenance staff to librarians.

Such attitude training should stress such things as the following:

- Awareness of the variety of special children, some of whom are *not* visually identifiable, and of their needs.
- Suspension of judgement. There is a great danger of making hasty estimations of intelligence based on external—behavioural—evidence. Gross physical behaviour (lack of control of bodily movement, for example) may mask high intelligence. Low intelligence may hide real, perhaps urgent, need for library service. Assumptions, for example, that deaf children will have no difficulty in reading, need to be critically examined, not uncritically accepted and acted upon. (Margaret Marshall (1981) points out that the prelingually deaf have considerable reading difficulties and need special, simplified, books).
- Suspension of reaction to 'unorthodox' appearance or behaviour. A look of horror, embarrassment, alarm, or pity may create a considerable barrier to the development of a productive, otherwise mutually-rewarding relationship.
- Positive approach and expectations. Knowing how far to protect and how far to challenge. Establishing what is acceptable, achievable, behaviour. For example, Margaret Marshall (1981, p.65) says that 'apart from sustained disruptive or deliberate offences, the librarian and other library users should be aware of and make allowances for the possibility of unusual noise in the library'. Those working with severely-handicapped youngsters will celebrate as landmarks advances that are barely perceptible to the uninitiated: 'Sally turned over the page on her own today!'
- Communication skills, not only those to meet the needs of the deaf and the unsighted but also those to obtain meaning from defective speech. If the community of deaf people is substantial, some members of staff should be prepared to learn to sign or finger-spell, or at least to be conscious of the requirements of lip-readers.

- Enjoyment of sharing, of mutual enjoyment and learning, which can take place with all kinds and conditions of children.
- Safety factors. A safe environment must be provided if the library is to cater for such vulnerable groups as the sight-impaired, the unco-ordinated, and the overactive.

The term 'special children' immediately brings to mind certain groups of children: those with limited or no sight who can be provided with materials in an appropriate form—books in large print, books to be read with trained finger-tips, books to be heard; those with hearing impairment who can fully utilize print and picture materials but who may not be given access to music (the value of such access is demonstrated by the career of the distinguished percussionist Evelyn Glennie). The mentally-handicapped, the brain damaged, and disturbed can enjoy books and picture material, and we have Dorothy Butler's heartening story of the multiply-handicapped Cushla (1979) to show what can be done through books and affection. The most severely-handicapped may be able to benefit from pictures and music, if they are given access to them. Less-obvious, but equally-important groups of 'special children' are the under-privileged, the withdrawn, and the gifted.

Children from the under-privileged sections of the community, the socially deprived, may well have been conditioned, even educated, to believe that they do not have access to such services as libraries. They may lack the confidence, the self-esteem, to venture into libraries. Here is a case for 'outreach' since, if the library is not shown to be hospitable and friendly by librarians going out to the children, the children are unlikely to make contact with the library in any way other than as vandals.

The library, with its traditional image of a quiet and unthreatening place, seems to be potentially receptive to unusually-shy, withdrawn, anxious, autistic, and similarly-emotionally disturbed young people. Here is a place that should offer security and privacy. Although libraries (especially young peoples' libraries) are not the havens of quiet of folk myth, they can cater for such children if staff are trained to recognize and respect them. Janet Hill (1973, p.69) says that 'Reading is essentially a private, personal activity, and in our anxiety to make sure children are finding what they want, we should not intrude on their privacy'. Service to shy and withdrawn youngsters may involve the art of leaving them alone, and of having the patience to wait until confidence and trust has been earned.

There has been limited provision for gifted children in the past. They have not always been given appropriate educational and library support. Indeed, they have not always been identified and have sometimes emerged not as gifted children but as problem, frustrated, children. The musically gifted have probably fared better than most. Quick to learn, quick to grasp concepts and to hypothesize, they need the best minds to provide appropriate support and challenge. The library would seem to provide much that these young people need, *if* the staff are alerted, are able to give time and informed attention, and are not slow to utilize material usually associated with adult readers.

In a limited treatment like this it is easy to be bland. There are considerable difficulties in working with children with special needs, and great devotion and expertise is required by those serving them. The fact remains, however, that they have a contribution to make to the community and that they have a right to our services. At least we should reduce those frustrating obstacles to obtaining services that are readily available to others, particularly those 'attitudinal obstacles' mentioned by Margaret Marshall (1981, p.66).

Bibliotherapy, which we might define as the systematic and informed use of reading in the treatment of psychological problems, requires a volume to itself and will not be developed here. That much reading has a therapeutic effect has been an argument throughout this book.

References and further reading

American Library Association (1956) *Patrons are people: how to be a model librarian*. Chicago, rev.edn.

Association of Assistant Librarians (1953) *The reader and the bookish manner*, London.

Ballinger, John (1903) 'Children's reading halls', *Library Association record*, Vol.5 pp.552 – 8.

Bettelheim, Bruno, and Zelan, Karen (1982) *On learning to read: the child's fascination with meaning*, London: Thames & Hudson.

Butler, Dorothy (1979) *Cushla and her books*, Sevenoaks: Hodder & Stoughton.

Donaldson, Margaret (1978) *Children's minds*, London: Fontana.

Elliott, Joyce (1982) 'Working with disturbed clients in libraries', *Communicator* (organ of the Librarians' Guild of Los Angeles Public Library), Vol.15, nos.1 – 2, pp.7 – 10.

Grotophorst, Clyde W. (1979) 'The problem patron: toward a comprehensive response', *Public library quarterly*, Vol.1, no.4, pp.345 – 53.

Harrod, Leonard Montague (1969) *Library work with children*, London: Andre Deutsch.

Hill, Janet (1973) *Children are people: the librarian in the community*, London: Hamish Hamilton.

'How to combat vandalism?' (1986), *Library Association record*, Vol.88, no.5, pp.229, 231.

Library Association (1983) *Code of professional conduct*. London, approved in September. (There is a useful set of *Guidance notes on the Code of professional conduct*, London: Library Association, March 1986.)

Library Association (1987) *Advice to members: Violence in libraries; preventing aggressive and unacceptable behaviour in libraries*, London.

McColvin, Lionel (1961) *Libraries for children*, London: Phoenix House.

MacLeod, Marcia (1986) 'Danger!', *Library Association record*, Vol.88, no.1, pp.23–4.

Marshall, Margaret R. (1981) *Libraries and the handicapped child*, London: André Deutsch.

Nottinghamshire County Library Service (1983) *Vandalism and unruly behaviour in libraries: a working party report*, Nottingham.

Sayers, W. C. Berwick (1932) *A manual of children's libraries*, London: Allen and Unwin.

Vogel, Betty (1976) 'The illegitimate patron', *Wilson library bulletin*, Vol.51, no.1, pp.65–6.

8

Managing the promotion of reading

This book has argued for the importance of reading, the contribution that what is read (and viewed and listened to) can make to the development of the assured, informed, and creative young person. If the argument is convincing then there is a need to convert that conviction into positive and practical activity.

Management is often seen as a cold, 'scientific', accountancy-dominated, limited, and limiting activity carried out by ruthlessly-ambitious young people in impressively-tailored suits. It is more useful, perhaps, to think in terms of 'creative management': to see management as the means of carrying out certain activities and of bringing about certain services. One needs dreams and visions but one also needs careful, practical thought to bring them into existence. Management, sound management, provides the means.

A policy for reading
Before rushing into a range of activities, an expenditure of staff time and materials, and of children's energies and colleagues' toleration, it is necessary to have a strategy for the promotion of reading, viewing, and listening—a clear idea of

- What we mean by reading, viewing, and listening;
- What we want to achieve, in the long term and the short term; and
- The range of possible means of achievement, bearing in mind cost and the availability of materials, expertise, accommodation, and equipment.

The initial step will be to consult the most appropriate people—parents, teachers, librarians, and other workers with young people. This may be done informally by interviewing, or formally by undertaking systematically-designed and structured interviews, library-user surveys, and community studies. The aim is to determine what is really needed, not merely what librarians or teachers *think* is needed. Adults come forward

97

willingly and confidently to pontificate about the needs of young people but their ideas sometimes arise out of needs that they remember as children, or from stereotypes (or romantic visions) of young people. They often show a failure to appreciate the present, to say nothing of the future, world in which young people live. The corrective is obvious but frequently overlooked: *to consult young people themselves.* Consultation involves establishing a relationship that clearly indicates the interviewees' ideas and opinions are to be given serious consideration, asking the right questions, accommodating new ideas introduced by the interviewee, and listening attentively and recording.

The aim is to produce a policy statement that includes as many of the ideas of those consulted as possible, that has been approved by as many as possible, and that can readily become the basis of a plan of action. The agreed policy should be liberally publicized.

Such a policy will, presumably, first of all present arguments justifying efforts to help young people to acquire, exercise, and improve those skills that will enable them to become critical—that is, questioning, appreciative, positive—readers, viewers, and listeners; skills that will also enable them to gain maximum information, knowledge, understanding, and enjoyment from a range of materials, from various kinds of books to sound recordings, films and videos, and computer software.

The policy would identify certain groups for whom the eventual activities and services are intended. Among such groups would be:

- pre-school children;
- those parenting pre-school children;
- pre-school play-group, nursery-school, and other leaders and teachers helping children before formal schooling;
- primary-school children;
- those parenting primary-school children;
- teachers of primary-school children, and their advisers and administrators;
- those providing after-school activities for primary-school-age children. Those concerned with sports and other leisure activities, with Beaver, Cub and Brownie groups, religious groups, etc.;
- secondary-school pupils;
- those parenting secondary-school pupils;
- teachers of secondary-school pupils, and their advisers and administrators;
- those providing after-school activities for secondary-school-age young people;

- young adults, whether undertaking education, working, or unemployed;
- children and young adults with special needs arising out of their intellectual ability, handicaps, ethnic or religious background, their parents' itinerant life-style, or whatever;
- those serving children and young adults with special needs by parenting, educating, providing leisure activities, and so on; and
- institutionalized children and young people, and the staff of such institutions providing educational and recreational and some medical services (such as bibliotherapy).

Such a policy, although mentioning such institutions as schools, hospitals, residential homes, and remand and youth custody centres for young offenders, would stress the need for a commitment to the individual young person and to his or her own needs, tastes, abilities, and limitations.

The resources
The range and quality of activities and services that can be offered by a particular library, or by co-operation between libraries and schools, for example, will depend upon the resources available. The basic resource is finance, and much of the manager's time and effort will be spent in gaining adequate funding, a fair share of public money, and, perhaps, sponsorship by industrial and commercial undertakings. The resources to be discussed are those resulting from this funding: stock, staff, accommodation, and the like.

Stock
It would be difficult to think of a successful reading-support programme that did not have as its foundation a sound collection of materials: a systematically-developed collection of books, periodicals, audio and visual tapes, slide collections, computer software, posters, toys and games, and similar materials.

In order to build up such a collection, over a period of years, it is necessary to have a collection policy, discussed, formulated, and publicized in a similar way to the policy for reading already considered in this chapter. Such a policy would cover the following:

1. *The aims and objectives of the collection* Basically, what it is for, what it is meant to support, and what the priorities are. Few collections are so liberally funded that they can provide everything for every user or group of users. Hence the need to determine agreed priorities. Those disadvantaged in some way, by low social status or mental or

physical handicap, for example, or those disadvantaged by having no alternative supply of materials, might be felt to have a higher priority than some other groups. Consideration should be given as well to the priorities of two extreme groups, non-readers who may be missing out in terms of enjoyment and information, and fluent, 'gifted' readers who may need specialized guidance with programmes of reading.

As can be seen, it is not possible to consider a collection without considering the community or communities, and the groups within those communities it is intended to serve.

2. *The scope of the collection* What subjects, languages, formats, and levels of comprehension will be covered? This is the opportunity to avoid endless controversy and *ad hoc*'ery by spelling out precisely what is included and what is excluded from the collection. Does the collection include sets of textbooks, plays, music, and so on? If there has been appropriate consultation and agreement, it can be shown that these policy decisions are group decisions, not the whim of some actual or imagined autocratic official such as 'The Librarian'.

3. *Controversial materials* Again, in order to avoid endless controversy, it is necessary to come to decisions about such important issues as sexual and ethnic stereotyping, practical books on the martial arts, explicit sexual descriptions, controversial pictorial material, the depiction of violence, the treatment of drugs, and so on.

If some materials are going to be withheld it is essential to be clear about *who* is being served by the restriction: vulnerable young people? Responsible parents? Overprotective parents? Troublesome pressure groups of adults? Is the withholding done to serve young people or merely to avoid a confrontation?

There should be an agreed and known procedure so that people are assured that complaints about specific materials are given serious, not merely token, consideration.

4. *Gifts* Does the acceptance of both solicited and unsolicited gifts imply that they will be put into the collection? That they will be displayed? That they will not be withdrawn? That other gifts from the same source will automatically receive the same treatment? There are so many religious, political, and commercial undertakings anxious to have publicity that it is necessary, in order to show impartiality and fair treatment, to have a clear and consistently-applied policy.

5. *Selection procedure and selection criteria* These should be given consideration in the policy. Yet again it is necessary to demonstrate that selection is carried out in a controlled, systematic, and consistent manner, and carried out by the most appropriate people. Depending upon the nature of the material, the most appropriate people might

be librarians, teachers, parents, and young people with particular specialisms and tastes.

6. *Collection maintenance* It is clear that if a collection is to remain up-to-date, relevant to the needs of those using it, and in decent physical condition, it must be constantly reviewed and 'edited'. A collection policy should cover such aspects of maintenance as 'weeding', replacement, and binding.

Stock maintenance is particularly important in collections that serve young people since

(a) much of the stock receives very heavy usage. Replacement of stock may account for one half to two-thirds of the bookfund;

(b) some of the stock is particularly vulnerable to damage in use, for example, pop-up and other activity books;

(c) there is a particular need for materials to *attract* use, and to set standards of quality;

(d) some of the most useful stock—that concerned with the latest cars and aircraft, fashions, musical tastes, world events, sport and so on—soon becomes out of date;

(e) young users tend to accept materials uncritically, assuming that what appears in all books, films, videos, and so on, is accurate and up to date.

It is important that a collection policy is seen as a set of guidelines rather than a set of directives. No policy can cover every eventuality. No policy can be expressed with such clarity and precision that its contents can be applied unthinkingly. Since a collection needs to reflect changes in the community, changes (for example) in educational thinking and ideas of good taste, no policy can remain useful unless it is critically reviewed and revised periodically.

The matter of selection criteria deserves further consideration. Selection criteria are applied when an item is being considered for addition to a collection, when an item is being considered for an award such as the Carnegie Medal or the Greenaway Medal, or when it is being considered for withdrawal from a collection.

In practice, the criteria being applied are within the mind of a seasoned selector who uses his or her professional expertise as teacher or librarian. Such selectors use their knowledge of the state of the collection they are developing, of the range of materials available ('bibliographical knowledge'), and of young people's tastes, interests, needs, and abilities.

Theoretically, selectors apply the sets of criteria that are published in the professional literature and that are formulated by individual library systems and schools. (There is an awe-inspiringly comprehensive set of criteria in Hicks and Tillin, 1972, pp.16−18. Many public library services have produced their own selection policy documents that contain selection criteria.) There is a value in discussing criteria, of bringing into consciousness those factors that are applied, or that might be applied, during selection. However, there are limits to the value of the resulting lists of criteria. First, they are too long to apply to every item under consideration: one set of criteria contains 47 factors for consideration! Second, they require the selector to have a God-like perception: an American example asks, among other things:

> Does the medium promote positive feeling toward all colors? [Reference here is to colours of the rainbow, not skin colour] . . .
> Does the medium foster the idea that the world of literature is fascinating? . . .
> Is the child's imaginative potential extended? . . .
> Does the medium help the child in his or her relationships with others? . . .
> Does the medium help the child perceive himself or herself in a positive manner?
>
> (Quisenberry, Shepherd, and Williams-Burns, 1973, p.38)

These *are* important questions but it is unlikely that positive answers would come readily to mind. It would even take considerable time and speculation to arrive at convincing predictions.

Many sets of criteria, while they investigate such details as, say, style, plot, and characterization, or factual accuracy, up-to-dateness, and language difficulty, fail to ask the fundamental questions:

- *What is the item attempting to do?* Good material usually provides an immediate answer. A preface, introduction, or 'blurb' will state clearly that it is written or designed to give certain information, at a certain level, to a particular readership. Other material can be seen to set out to stimulate discussion, or entertain, or give insight and understanding. It is sometimes difficult to arrive at what an item is attempting to do beyond achieving maximum sales.
- *Is what it is attempting to do relevant to the needs of our particular group of young people?* This consideration will take into account not only the needs, wants, interests, and tastes of the young people but also the policy of the library within the philosophy of the parent organization or community, such as public-library system or school.
- *Is there evidence that it is likely to succeed in its aim?* This is the point where most sets of criteria become relevant.

Fiction presents more evaluation difficulties than information books for the obvious reason that it is written and read subjectively. Various attempts have been made to produce sets of criteria, some verging on the ludicrous. Philip Larkin's personal set of criteria (1983, p.94) produced when he was concerned with the Booker Award in 1977, is more useful than most. He asked the following of a novel:

Could I read it?
If I could read it, did I believe it?
If I believed it, did I care about it?
And if I cared about it, what was the quality of my caring, and would it last?

This list of questions has more virtue than that of brevity: it is a reminder that the evaluation of a novel or a story is essentially personal and subjective. A really successful novel, which may not necessarily be a commercially-successful novel, engages the reader in a particularly powerful and penetrating way. A very successful novel or story makes slight or even substantial changes in the reader's understanding, perceptions, and approach to life. It, to some extent, rewrites the reader.

The final point about criteria is that most materials select themselves. Exciting books like Anthony Browne's *Gorilla*, and stunning and disturbing films like Nicolas Roeg's version of *Walkabout*, cry out for acquisition, while poor and mediocre materials cause a mere shrugging of the selector's shoulders. On the few occasions when the experienced selector is perplexed there are others (professional colleagues and informed young people) to consult. If all else fails one can await the reviewers' verdicts.

All of the foregoing assumes that selectors have learned 'The "Peppermint" lesson' (Moss, 1986).

Staff
As is stressed in Chapter 7, the keys to the success or failure of services and activities are the attitudes and experience of the staff, particularly the attitudes demonstrated when any potential user approaches 'the library' or 'the school', or wherever the programme is taking place. 'The school' or 'the library' may be seen as the building or as represented by the first member of the institution encountered. Ensuring positive attitudes is, as is discussed earlier, a matter of careful staff selection and of staff training.

Accommodation
The accommodation may be viewed as those areas in which activities and services can be offered. There is a need for areas for such activities as story-telling sessions, drama, music making, film showing, and so on.

There is a need for areas where young people can use library materials and talk: reading and talking are not seen as alternative activities by most young people. There should be areas for quiet, but it is rarely necessary to require silence: sepulchres are high on silence but low on positive stimulation.

Accommodation may also be seen in terms of creating an appropriate environment for those activities appropriate in a library. In the late 1960s Norman Beswick (1969, pp.5−6) defined the library in a school or college in the terms of 'A learning environment, artfully designed to have a stimulating and enriching effect upon students; it uses the strategy of individual, independent study and enquiry, provoked in a variety of ways, to have this effect'. This, with perhaps a little adjustment to make it 'a learning and entertaining environment', could be applied to any library serving young people. It makes the important point that everything within the library (from well-designed furniture and fittings, paintings and sculpture, display and availability of the varied stock of materials, and the staff attitudes and concern for 'good-housekeeping') should produce a welcoming, interesting, and usable ('user-friendly') atmosphere. A successful library is full of those things that should arouse curiosity and also those things and persons who will help the individual to satisfy that curiosity. The attitude and behaviour of those using the services and taking part in the activities will also, of course, contribute to or corrode that atmosphere. The latter point is discussed in Chapter 7.

Other resources
There are other resources besides stock, staff, and accommodation that will need to be available if certain activities are to take place or services are to be provided. These include secretarial help, audio-visual technicians, graphic designers and display artists, and photocopying and printing facilities. These are sometimes overlooked at the early stages of planning.

The other major resources are 'allies', that is, sympathetic and supportive helpers such as teachers, parents, specialists, enthusiasts, and performers of various kinds—and co-operative, talented, or merely cheerful and willing young people.

The means
Among the means of promoting reading, viewing, and listening, the following might be considered:

● Provision of information about books and related materials. The librarian, aided by a range of printed and computer services, is the community's bibliographical (materiographical?) expert and should, with proper publicity, be recognized as such. In the spirit of informal education, one would like to see librarians as reading tutors offering advice on sequences of reading—not merely the next title to read in the sequence after *The dark is rising*, but what materials to use, in what order, to build up an understanding of, say, Ancient Greece, or the sea birds of Britain, or of geology.

- Support for learner-readers, their parents and their teachers. This would need to be based upon a sound understanding of what happens in the reading programmes in local schools, and would take the form of provision of materials and of providing channels of communication for the sharing of experience and the giving of advice.

- Support for the personal ownership of things like books, sound recordings such as story tapes and music, and of videos like *The snowman* and *The railway children*. The Bullock report of 1975 stressed the responsibility of schools in promoting book purchase by displays, by running school bookshops, and by encouraging membership of book clubs (DES, 1975, para.7.5). Donald Fry (1985, p.96) has shown that such ownership has an important role to play in the process of building up personal identity: 'What we choose to read, or simply the books we choose to have in our possession, are indications of the ways we want to be seen and the ways we see ourselves'.

  Merely to make young people aware of the range of materials available, the range of paperbacks and of audio-tapes and videos, serves a valuable purpose. This is especially so in areas where there are no bookshops, or where bookshops display only a very limited range of materials.

- Provision of a range of inspired and carefully-managed activities for the learner and the competent reader. Activities would be planned to demonstrate the range of materials available; to give guidance in the enjoyment of a range of audio, visual, and reading experiences; and to provide opportunities for young people to share such experiences and to talk about them. Reading, listening to music, and watching plays or films are often thought of as solitary activities, but an essential element of the enjoyment is discussion after the experience. What was the novelist/playwright/programme-maker trying to do? Was the behaviour of the characters convincing? What would *you* have done? What were the issues raised and how were they discussed? How do you 'get into' a story (Karnail's problem in Fry, 1985, Ch.5)? How do you listen to, and bring meaning to, certain kinds of music?

- Provision for creative activity. One result of a programme may be to convert some listeners, viewers, and readers into writers, performers, or creators, partly because one of the best ways to learn (to learn to appreciate, for example) is to do, and partly because many young people are unaware of their own creative abilities—there is a need to provide opportunities to practise and to perform. Hence the need to have the guidance and support of such people as writers, musicians, film-makers, painters, print-makers, model-makers, and such like 'in residence'.

Publicity

An essential element of any organization is to make known what it has available, where and when. Libraries should not assume that all their intended users know the range of materials, advice, services, activities, and accommodation they offer. Nor should they assume that those intended users have the image of a modern, bright, welcoming library, staffed by welcoming people. Publicity is intended to affect expectations as well as present information.

Publicity is, of course, expensive (of staff time as much as anything else) and so it must be effective. It should extend beyond the immediate environment of the library or school to the wider community where, for example, the parents and the pre-school children live and work. The local newspapers, television, and radio stations are as important as the posters and leaflets.

An ulterior motive for publicity is to give the library or school a 'higher profile' so that it attracts funds and interested people (the 'allies' previously mentioned as valuable resources in the community).

Evaluation

In accordance with sound management principles, every activity and service needs to be carefully assessed in terms of the degree and cost of achievement. Should the activity or service continue? Could it be improved? This evaluation should include everything from an impromptu story-telling session ('There are plenty of children around. I wonder if they would like a story?'), to a series of ethnic arts festivals. Such assessment would include staff involvement: the cost of providing—or failing to provide—staff with particular expertise, experience, and personalities.

There is a fundamental problem in the evaluation of activities and services: how is their effectiveness to be measured? One can measure the investment cost of time and money fairly accurately but what is the 'product' and what is its value? In these terms, evaluation is impossible. The aim, perhaps, is to produce a group of young people who are better informed, confident, and competent to obtain information, understanding, and entertainment from the materials provided. The result may not show immediately. It may not be measurable in crude terms of extra library borrowing.

In practice, evaluation will probably take the form of subjective but informed assessment of the success or otherwise of a service or activity. It may be 'unscientific' but it will be the careful evaluation that is the daily professional activity of librarians and teachers. It will be professional in that certain objectives will have been set, certain factors will have been isolated for observation beforehand, and evaluation (in terms of the degree of the achievement of the objectives) will be a planned and essential element of the whole enterprise.

Evaluation is one of those processes that not only has to be carried out but has also to be seen to be carried out. It is an outward and visible sign of sound management activity. It is a continuous process to be carried out not merely at the end of an activity or period of time but also during the running of an event or process. Its purpose is to measure, perhaps crudely, the degree of achievement of aims and objectives and to indicate when anything has to be improved, rethought, or 'junked'. Perhaps the original objectives were too ambitious, perhaps they were not ambitious enough. Continuing evaluation may indicate that alterations need to be made. There is little point in continuing a mistaken course if changing it can save money and human enthusiasm and effort.

Evaluations can have publicity value, and fund-supporting value, if they are used in some form of annual or other report. If they are not discussed, or acted upon, or 'published' in some way, the value of evaluations is lost and important issues are not being raised.

The basic question needs to be asked, and asked periodically: why are we doing what we are doing? For the glory of the institution? To give ourselves a nice, warm glow? To show fellow professionals that we are here? Or to help to produce and to support what Aidan Chambers (1983, p.5) has called 'willing, avid, and responsive readers of literature'—and readers of 'rubbish' and enjoyers of music and film and television and, well, life.

References and further reading

Beswick, Norman (1969) 'Bookstore—or media center?: some American answers', *Education libraries bulletin*, no.35, pp.1 – 18.

Chambers, Aidan (1983) *Introducing books to children*, London: Heinemann, 2nd edn.

DES (1975) *A language for life*, the Bullock report, London.: HMSO.

Fry, Donald (1985) *Children talk about books: seeing themselves as readers*, Milton Keynes: Open University Press.

Hicks, Warren B., and Tillin, Alma M. (1972) *Developing multi-media libraries*, New York: R. R. Bowker.

Larkin, Philip (1983) *Required writing: miscellaneous pieces, 1955—1982*, London: Faber & Faber.

Moss, Elaine (1986) 'The "Peppermint" lesson' in her *Part of the pattern: a personal journey through the world of children's books, 1960—1985*, London: The Bodley Head, pp.33—4.

Quisenberry, Nancy L., Shepherd, Terry R., and Williams-Burns, Winona (1973) 'Criteria for the selection of records, filmstrips and films for young children', *Audiovisual instructor*, Vol.18, no.4, pp.36, 38.

9

The future of reading

The discussion in this book has argued for the importance of reading *now*, much of it assuming a future for reading—at least reading print. This assumption seems more assured than it did. In the early stages of the multi-media revolution it was suggested that reading and books were superseded. Reading print was somehow unnatural; looking and listening were basic human activities. We were in an audio-visual age that had returned those basics to humanity. Reading and books were redundant. Then the multi-media revolution was itself overtaken by information technology, which relegated many of the projectors of sound and image to museum shelves close to the magic lanterns, zoetropes, and cylinder gramophones. Video discs, teletexts, computer systems, and their like, have revolutionized the revolution.

At this stage one can foresee the end of the book in its present form, but its present form—the printed codex—is anyway historically quite a recent arrival. Indeed, the whole idea of 'recording' is also new when related to story-telling and oral tradition. The book may disappear but the words remain, and words to be read have to appear somewhere. They have appeared on clay tablets, on papyrus rolls, and in hand-written and printed books. It would seem that most of them are now appearing on VDUs, in thousands, millions, of words, figures, and images. They have to be *read*, that is, decoded and understood and acted upon.

Computer systems
What are these systems producing to be read? Masses and masses of data, calculations, graphics to teach, to support research and the development of new ideas, new processes, new techniques in engineering, medicine, and so on. They are making it easier to carry out financial transactions, to book seats on planes and in theatres, to buy goods, and to invest more safely.

Computer systems are in the schools, teaching and enabling exploration and learning. They are helping young people to cope with, to take part in, and to benefit from an age of constant change, constant scientific and technological advancement.

Is there nothing these systems will not do? At the moment they are poor at replacing reading matter and the need to read. They are also poor at helping people to understand people and individual people to understand themselves. A surprising number of systems, such as those in banks, can cope with people only if people reduce themselves to simple, limited machines. We have not always received the systems we need. In school education, for example, Beswick (1987, p.5) has warned that 'Too heavy a reliance on a technology which emphasizes sequential learning, instrumental thinking, and an educational method based on the finding of answers known to exist, rather than sought and created, may lead to a lop-sided emphasis in our system'.

Systems are still largely concerned with the controllable, and that excludes a great deal of human behaviour. Systems are, currently at least, weak in enabling the exploration of the closest and most problematic subject—*ourselves*, as human beings and as individuals.

At this stage of human advancement, of breathtakingly-swift and revolutionary advancement in many spheres, much of the discussion, the data, the prophecy, the planning, and the opinion is expressed and communicated in print, in books and periodical articles and reports, and in printouts and displays that have to be read. Human experience, news, and flight-departure times appear in print. The illiterate person, the person who cannot read, is more powerless today than ever before in history.

Reading in schools

The teaching of reading in schools has not become less important but has been transformed. With the new emphasis on information-handling skills (on the skills of information acquiring, information processing, information evaluation, and information presentation) reading is now a matter of concern throughout the whole of a young person's school life, and the emphasis is on what might be called 'real reading', that is, critical, questioning reading, reading for meaning.

This new emphasis came with the introduction of the dreaded 'project work' into schools, and the encouragement of individual enquiry and discovery. Often under-planned and under-directed, the aims were left vague and the pupils reduced the process to mechanical, laborious copying-out, made respectable and rewarded by good visual presentation. (The author remembers seeing a primary-school project that appeared to reflect a considerable knowledge of microbiology on the part of the pupil. It was highly graded, perhaps by a teacher who was not in a position to examine the post-graduate material offered.)

Times have changed. The teacher of information skills now has precise objectives, a clear view of what he or she is aiming to achieve. Outlining her work in the primary school, Pat Avann (1985, p.2) identifies a sequence of information activities:

1) identifying a need for information and being able to articulate that need (what do I want to know?)
2) framing appropriate questions (how can I find out?)
3) finding information sources (where do I find out?)
4) evaluating information sources (will they answer my questions? how reliable are they?)
5) extracting relevant information (this is what I need to know)
6) processing and, if necessary, presenting the information found to satisfy the original need or to convince others (this is what I've found out).

Translating this into classroom work it is easy to see that any but the competent reader are going to be handicapped heavily. The new educational emphases, evident in the work of the primary schools and the GCSE and the Education Reform Act, that reflect the value of information-holding and handling in our society, are giving more, and not less, attention to the importance of reading.

At the same time, parents have a more central role to play in helping their children to become competent readers. The partnership between teachers, parents, and children in reading programmes has proved to be very successful—a mutually-rewarding process involving encouragement of private reading as well as 'public' reading, book sharing, and book ownership.

Perhaps the emphasis on information-handling has been at the cost of assistance in reading stories, novels, and poetry ('imaginative literature'). There is still a need for such material, however, and Donald Fry's study *Children talk about books* (1985) provides us with ways of observing and sharing experience with young readers. It also indicates sensitive ways of working with the young reader in the classroom.

Young people, if they are to be prepared for the opportunities of the future, need to be able to handle information; and young people, if they are to cope with the challenges of the future, will still need to explore their own individuality, will need to learn to live with themselves and to learn to live (in a variety of relationships) with others.

In the past, along with the appreciation of the values of reading books, has gone a sort of reverence, for the book: all books, regardless of the nature and quality of the text. With this has gone an undervaluing of such media as sound recordings, films, and videos. This is in despite of the fact that the book has grave limitations in communicating sound—music, the human voice, animal sounds, and industrial sounds. Attempts to convey bird song in print, for example, were brave but tended towards the ludicrous. Older editions of *The Observer's book of birds* tell us that the little owl produces 'a mewing "qui", "quee-eet" or "ki-wak", and a snore', and the bearded tit a ' "cht, cht", and a twanging "ping" '. Similarly, the printed word and the still picture could only convey a limited idea of movement, whether ballet and dance, or human, animal, or mechanical movement.

Now, with a range of technology, it is possible and desirable to think in terms of the most appropriate medium, or set of media, for a particular task, whether that task is to enable someone to study the work of the mason, or the life of the cheetah, or the world of Ernest Shepard.

Television

Television is the medium that dominates the mass communication of our own time and its familiarity and availability have caused it to be undervalued: there is so much of it, with numerous channels pouring out a range of programmes with a wide range of quality. Much of it appears to be 'bad' (mindless, routine, numbingly inoffensive); much of it is of a very high quality in terms of content and technical quality. More attention seems to be given to the bad and the 'damaging' (all the 'sex and violence' that politicians and protectors of decency seem to be able to find), than to the good and the outstanding. One factor, video-recording, should have brought a change of attitude in that the idea of television as an ephemeral medium has to be modified. What is thought to be useful or worth while can now be kept and made available to be viewed when required.

There is an educational task here to encourage a more-considered approach to television, initially in having programmes *looked at* and discussed rather than merely seen. There is a problem in that we lack the 'critical approach', the critical apparatus, to deal with television. As Fiske and Hartley have pointed out (1978, p.15), television cannot be treated as an alternative form of literary text since it owes more to conversation than to the printed word. It is immediate, lively, companionable, and frequently trivial and ephemeral. It engages you as an individual rather than as an 'audience', yet it invites you to sit alone in your room, your play-pen, or your corner of the sofa, to join in with an electronic community: the *Rainbow* group, the *Play School* group, the *Blue Peter* group, or the *Wide Awake Club*. It deluges with a seemingly-endless chatter and the movement and funny noises of animated cartoons. It also offers imaginative adaptations of books and stories, original plays and series, story-telling and nursery rhymes, and inventive presentation of science and design ideas. It is, in short, a rich resource that sometimes soothes (for the after-school calm down, perhaps), sometimes stimulates, and sometimes provides the familiar stuff of playground conversation.

It also needs to be said that television cannot be treated as if it were the same as film. This becomes clear when one sees the film version of a television series. As film, the familiar television material becomes slower, too spacious, and so less intimate. Caution is necessary if one attempts to apply the 'critical apparatus' of the cinema to television programmes.

Since young people are so exposed to and influenced by television, those working with them must be familiar with what they are viewing—not merely 'children's television' but also the adverts and the adult programmes they are viewing. The magic nine-o'clock barrier between family viewing and adult viewing exists only in the minds of those who have no contact with young people and their way of life.

If young people see too much sex and violence, they also see acted out (along with the excesses) a range of loving—and loathing—relationships; they see the realities of violence as well as the false, hygienic, violence of *The A Team*. They need to talk through what they have seen and not be rushed through to the next cartoon or talk show. They need to discuss why people behave as they do. More basically, they need to be made aware of what is actually happening, as distinct from what is being shown. They need the opportunity to decide what is good about a programme and what is superficial or false.

Young viewers need to be reminded that the television world is not the real world. They may be made aware of this: some children will find that their own cultural group is under-represented, or the occupational group of their parents is under-represented (when did you last see a brick-layer, or a convincing portrayal of a clergyman on television?). They are, however, less unlikely than formerly to see their social class represented but they may be very lucky to see their local culture represented unless they live in parts of London or Merseyside.

Such discussion should, perhaps, take place in the home, but this rarely happens. It takes place in the playground but tends to be limited and undirected. There is, it can readily be argued, a case for teachers and librarians to help young people to discuss their viewing. The aim is to assist in the creation of critical and appreciative television viewers; in short, an increase in the enjoyment of television (see Masterman, 1985 and McMahon and Quin, 1986, for further approaches to teaching television appreciation).

The cinema
Before television, the dominant medium of entertainment was the cinema. Until recently one might have been forgiven for overlooking films, as

the cinema seemed to have lost the struggle for survival. The unexpected revival of cinema owes more than a little to its audience of young people. It is they, the television generation, who have returned to the cinema in great numbers. Perhaps, after watching the small box in the living-room, they are the ones to appreciate the sense of occasion (a night out at the pictures), the large picture and the spaciousness (*2001: a space odyssey* failed on the small screen), the special effects, and the pleasures of being part of a live, responding audience.

The revival of the popular film has been brought about, largely, by a succession of space fantasies, such as the *Star wars* films, by fantasy films using the material of myth and legend, such as *The never-ending story*, *The dark crystal*, and *Labyrinth*, and by the return of the boys' adventure stories such as the *Indiana Jones* films. The local cinema, where one exists, is on young people's maps: it is a place they go.

Much cinema has been elevated to fine art, the critical appreciation of films being established—much of it being substantial and useful (some of it is, however, pretentious and foolish). Few seem to have made the effort to develop appreciation skills among young people (but see Monaco, 1981, McMahon and Quin, 1986, and the publications of the British Film Institute), which seems unfortunate considering the obvious enjoyment young people obtain from films.

If teachers, librarians, and others are concerned about the quality of reading, viewing, and listening, it does seem appropriate that they take an interest in making the best available and in providing opportunities to develop understanding and enjoyment of the cinema.

Suppression, restriction, promotion

There is another aspect of the future of reading, viewing, and listening that needs to be acknowledged, and that is the matter of the withholding of access to information and materials.

The vision of *Fahrenheit 451* (Bradbury, 1957) has not come about. In his SF story, Ray Bradbury saw a world in which books were burned because they were seen to threaten a society that valued non-reflective conformity, immediate rewards, perpetual comfort, and undisturbed peace-of-mind. Books, and particularly the ideas in books, are disturbing: questioning, disrupting, and challenging. 'You ask Why to a lot of things and you wind up very unhappy indeed, if you keep at it' (*ibid*. p.64). Hence the need for the firemen, 'The Happiness Boys', the book burners.

The distrust and control in *Fahrenheit 451* has not come about although there have been, and there remain, large-scale attempts at suppression—of Jewish and Communist materials by the Nazis, of non-Communist ideas by the Stalin regime, and so on. Even a freedom-loving country such as

Britain becomes sensitive when there is the possibility of the publication of information about the secret service, homosexual behaviour, disclosures about the captains of cricket teams, and other matters of national concern.

Most people who suppress material or who limit access to material find good reasons for doing so. It is 'not in the national interest' to have access to and discussion of certain matters. There are sections of the community who may be damaged by too early exposure, or any exposure, to certain ideas or acts. Some books, films, and videos contain deeply-depressing, anti-life, anti-hope views of human beings. Why offend 'good taste'?

A major group who need (or seem to need) protection, are young people. Some children are vulnerable: the insecure, the abused, the neglected, and the unloved, among others. And there are materials that *in our judgement* (and there sounds the danger signal) contain wrong values, offer the wrong models, and that are vague or misleading about these essential matters.

It would be impossible, however, to protect young people from all that is negative, dated, and undesirable—the bad, the mediocre, and the misguided. Indeed, it might not prove possible to reach agreement as to what *is* bad, mediocre, and misguided. It is also worth remembering that young people, as well as adults, encounter the undesirable in reality, in the home, in the street and the playground, as well as indirectly through books, television programmes, and films.

Most young people, especially those guided and encouraged, have developed faculties of discrimination. They perceive and judge people and their behaviour and attitudes, they take psychological temperatures and 'read' emotional situations all day long. They evaluate television programmes, films, books, and magazines. They often have highly-developed senses that identify the true and the false, the sincere and the shamming.

The work of teachers, librarians, and parents is to recognize the existence and the importance of these developing skills, and to help in their growth and in their confident application, to allow the development of and to recognize the value of young people's opinions.

Rather than concentrate on negative aspects of materials, it seems preferable to promote 'the best'—and 'the good' and 'the best' in terms of the needs and abilities of the individual young person; to provide opportunities to have a range of sound, image, and print experiences, and experiences through live performance as well as recorded performance; to offer a wide range of experiences that are exciting, revealing, provocative, stimulating, giggle-making, breathtaking, and life-enhancing; and to offer opportunities for the development of those skills and insights—skills and insights that are needed if one is to obtain the fullest possible meaning from print, sound, and pictures. The rewards are understanding and enjoyment: a lifetime of growth and development.

References and further reading
Avann, Pat (ed.) (1985) *Teaching information skills in the primary school*, London: Edward Arnold.
Beswick, Norman (1987) *Re-thinking active learning 8−16*, London: The Falmer Press.
Bradbury, Ray (1957) *Fahrenheit 451*, London: Corgi.
Fiske, John, and Hartley, John (1978) *Reading television*, London: Methuen.
Fry, Donald (1985) *Children talk about books: seeing themselves as readers*, Milton Keynes: Open University Press.
McMahon, Barrie, and Quin, Robyn (1986) *Real images: film and television*, South Melbourne: Macmillan. (Provides an approach and a structure for the teaching of television programme appreciation. Clearly relevant to work with older young people, it could provide the basis for television work with younger age groups. Also covers film.)
Masterman, Len (1985) *Teaching the media*, London: Comedia. (See comment to McMahon and Quin, 1986, above.)
Monaco, James (1981) *How to read a film: the art, technology, language, history, and theory of film and media*. New York and Oxford: Oxford University Press, rev.edn.

A brief reading list:
Children's authors and books
mentioned in the text

(Note that the date of the first English edition is given, followed by the hardback publisher, and finally the paperback edition publisher. In those cases where no specific book is mentioned in the text, an example of the author's work is included in the bibliography. Remember that these are books mentioned in the text and are not necessarily recommendations for young readers. Readers in the USA will find that there are variations in the publishers, and occasionally changes of title, in the American editions of the books listed. Such readers should check details in the current edition of *Children's books in print*, published by R. R. Bowker.)

Adams, Richard, *Watership Down*, 1972. Allen Lane/Puffin.
Ahlberg, Janet and Ahlberg, Allan, *The baby's catalogue*, 1982. Kestrel/Picture Puffin.
Ahlberg, Janet and Ahlberg, Allan, *The ha ha bonk book*, 1982. Kestrel/Puffin.
Ahlberg, Janet and Ahlberg, Allan, *The old joke book*, 1987. Kestrel/Puffin.
Alcott, Louisa May, *Little women*, 1868. Numerous editions.
Ardizzone, Edward, The little Tim books. Oxford University Press/ Puffin.
Barrie, J. M., *Peter Pan*, 1911. Numerous editions.
Baum, L. Frank, *The wizard of Oz*, 1900. Numerous editions.
Bell, J. T., *Wee MacGreegor*. No HB/Panther [collected newspaper stories].
Blackmore, R. D., *Lorna Doone*, 1869. Numerous editions.
Blake, Quentin, *Mister Magnolia*, 1980. Cape/Picture Lions.
Blume, Judy, *It's not the end of the world*, 1979. Heinemann/Piccolo.
Blyton, Enid, *Five go to Mystery Moor*, 1954. Hodder/Knight Books.
Blyton, Enid, *Five have plenty of fun*, 1955. Hodder/Knight Books.
Blyton, Enid, *Look out Secret Seven*, 1962. Hodder/Knight Books.
Blyton, Enid, *Well done, Secret Seven*, 1951. Hodder/Knight Books.
Boston, Lucy, The Green Knowe books, 1954−64. Faber/Puffin.

Briggs, Raymond, *Fungus the bogeyman*, 1977. Hamish Hamilton/ Hamish Hamilton.

Briggs, Raymond, *The snowman*, 1973. Hamish Hamilton/Picture Puffin.

Briggs, Raymond, *When the wind blows*, 1982. Hamish Hamilton/ Penguin.

Brown, Jeff, *Flat Stanley*, 1968. Methuen/Magnet.

Browne, Anthony, *Gorilla*, 1983. Julia McRae/Magnet.

Bruna, Dick, *b is for bear*, 1967. Methuen/no PB.

Bunyan, John, *The pilgrim's progress*, 1678. Numerous editions.

Burnett, Frances Hodgson, *The secret garden*, 1911. Numerous editions.

Burningham, John, *ABC*, 1964. Cape/no PB.

Burton, Hester, *Time of trial*, 1963. Oxford University Press/no PB.

Byars, Betsy, *Cracker Jackson*, 1985. Bodley Head/Puffin.

Carroll, Lewis, The Alice books. Numerous editions.

Christopher, John, *The guardians*, 1970. Hamish Hamilton/Puffin.

Clarke, Pauline, *The twelve and the genii*, 1962. Faber/Bodley Head.

Cooper, Clare, *The black horn*, 1982. Hodder/no PB.

Cooper, Susan, *The dark is rising* novels, 1965−77. Chatto & Windus/ Puffin.

Crompton, Richmal, The William stories. Macmillan/Macmillan.

Dahl, Roald, *The enormous crocodile*, 1978. Cape/Picture Puffin.

Defoe, Daniel, *Robinson Crusoe*, 1719. Numerous editions.

Eastman, P. D., *Are you my mother?*, 1962. Collins/Collins.

Farrar, Frederic W., *Eric, or, little by little*, 1858. No edition in print.

Fisk, Nicholas, *Sweets from a stranger*, 1982. Kestrel/Puffin.

Ga'g, Wanda, *Millions of cats*, 1929. Faber/Puffin.

Garfield, Leon, *Smith*, 1967. Constable/Puffin.

Garfield, Leon, *The strange affair of Adelaide Harris*, 1971. Longman/ Puffin.

Garner, Alan, *The Weirdstone of Brisingamen*, 1960. Collins/Fontana Lions.

Grahame, Kenneth, *The wind in the willows*, 1908. Numerous editions.

'Grey Owl', *The adventures of Sajo and her beaver people*, 1935. Heinemann/no PB.

Harnett, Cynthia, *The load of unicorn*, 1959. Methuen/Puffin.

Henty, G. A., *At Aboukir and Acre*, 1899. Blackie & Son.

Hoban, Russell, *How Tom beat Captain Najork and his hired sportsmen*, 1974. Cape/Picture Puffin.

Hughes, Shirley, *Dogger*, 1977. Bodley Head/Picture Lions.

Hughes, Shirley, *Up and up*, 1979. Bodley Head/Picture Lions.

Hutchins, Pat, *Rosie's walk*, 1970. Bodley Head/Picture Puffin.

Jansson, Tove, The Moomin books, 1950−1971. Benn/Puffin.

Kearton, Cherry, *My animal friendships*, 1932. No edition in print.

Kemp, Gene, *The turbulent term of Tyke Tiler*, 1977. Faber/Puffin.

Kingsley, Charles, *The water babies*, 1863. Various editions.

Lawrence, Louise, *Children of the dust*, 1985. Bodley Head/Bodley Head.

Lear, Edward, *The complete nonsense*, 1947. Faber/no PB.

L'Engle, Madeleine, *Meet the Austins*, 1966. Collins/Fontana Lions.

L'Engle, Madeleine, *A swiftly tilting planet*, 1978. Souvenir Press/no PB.

L'Engle, Madeleine, *A wrinkle in time*, 1963. Constable/Puffin.

Lewis, C. S., The Narnia books, 1950−56. Geoffrey Bles/Fontana Lions.

Lindgren, Astrid, The Pippi Longstocking books. Oxford University Press/Oxford University Press.

Lindsay, Norman, *The magic pudding*, 1931. Angus & Robertson/Puffin.

Lingard, Joan, *The gooseberry*, 1978. Hamish Hamilton/Beaver.

MacDonald, George, *At the back of the north wind*, 1871. Numerous editions.

Mark, Jan, *Handles*, 1983. Kestrel/Puffin.

Marryat, Frederick, *The children of the New Forest*, 1847. Numerous editions.

Masefield, John, *The box of delights*, 1935. Heinemann/Puffin.

Masefield, John, *The midnight folk*, 1927. Heinemann/Puffin.

Milne, A. A., *The house at Pooh Corner*, 1928. Methuen/Methuen.

Nesbit, E., *The railway children*, 1906. Dent/Puffin.

Norton, Mary, The Borrowers stories, 1975−1982. Dent/Puffin.

Noyes, Alfred, *The highwayman*, illustrated by Charles Keeping, 1981. Oxford University Press/Oxford University Press.

Orwell, George, *Animal farm*, 1945. Numerous editions.

Oxford book of poetry for children, illustrated by Brian Wildsmith, 1963. Oxford University Press/Oxford University Press.

Pearce, Philippa, *Tom's midnight garden*, 1958. Oxford University Press/Puffin.

Peyton, K. M., The Flambards novels, 1967−9. Oxford University Press/Puffin.

Peyton, K. M., *The right-hand man*, 1977. Oxford University Press/Oxford University Press.

Potter, Beatrix, *The tale of the Flopsy Bunnies*, 1909. Warne/no PB.

Potter, Beatrix, *The tale of Peter Rabbit*, 1902. Warne/no PB.

Ransome, Arthur, *Winter holiday*, 1933. Cape/Puffin.

Sendak, Maurice, *In the night kitchen*, 1971. Bodley Head/Picture Puffin.

Seton, Ernest Thompson, *Wild animals I have known*, 1898. No HB/ Penguin.

Southall, Ivan, *Josh*, 1971. Angus & Robertson/Puffin.

Stevenson, Robert Louis, *Treasure island*, 1883. Numerous editions.

Sutcliff, Rosemary, *The eagle of the ninth*, 1954. Oxford University Press/Puffin.

Swift, Jonathan, *Gulliver's travels*, 1726. Numerous editions.

Swindells, Robert, *Brother in the land*, 1984. Oxford University Press/ Puffin.

Tolkien, J. R. R., *The hobbit*, 1937. Allen & Unwin/Allen & Unwin.

Tolkien, J. R. R., *The lord of the rings*, 1954−5. Allen & Unwin/ Allen & Unwin.

Townsend, John Rowe, *Gumble's yard*, 1961. Hutchinson/Puffin.

Treece, Henry, *Horned helmet*,1970. Hodder/Puffin.

Twain, Mark, *The adventures of Huckleberry Finn*, 1884. Numerous editions.

Twain, Mark, *The adventures of Tom Sawyer*, 1876. Numerous editions.

Walsh, Jill Paton, *A parcel of patterns*, 1983. Kestrel/Puffin.

White, E. G., *Charlotte's web*, 1952. Hamish Hamilton/Puffin.

White, T. H., *Mistress Masham's repose*, 1947. Cape/Puffin.

Willard, Barbara, *Ned only*, 1985. Julia MacRae/Magnet.

Zolotow, Charlotte, *Mr Rabbit and the lovely present*, illustrated by Maurice Sendak, 1968. Bodley Head/Picture Puffin.

Index

127